"INDIAN" STEREOTYPES IN TV SCIENCE FICTION

"INDIAN" STEREOTYPES
IN TV SCIENCE FICTION

First Nations' Voices Speak Out

BY SIERRA S. ADARE

 University of Texas Press, Austin

Much of the material in Chapter 2 was previously published in "Colonial-Era Stereotypes of Indigenous Peoples Remain in the 2000s," *Red Ink,* 2001 special double issue on "Indian" stereotyping (volume 9.2/10.1), courtesy University of Arizona.

Printed in the United States of America
First edition, 2005

Requests for permission to reproduce
material from this work should be sent to:
Permissions
University of Texas Press
P.O. Box 7819
Austin, TX 78713-7819.

⊗ The paper used in this book meets the
minimum requirements of ANSI/NISO
Z39.48-1992 (R1997) (Permanence of Paper).

Library of Congress Cataloging-in-Publication Data
Adare, Sierra.
  "Indian" stereotypes in TV science fiction : First Nations' voices speak out / by Sierra S. Adare. — 1st ed.
     p.   cm.
  Includes bibliographical references and index.
  ISBN 0-292-70611-1 (cl. : alk. paper) —
  ISBN 0-292-70612-X (pbk. : alk. paper)
  1. Indians on television.   2. Science fiction television programs—United States.   I. Title.
  PN1992.8.I64A32   2005
  791.45′652997—dc22
                                        2004021223

ᎣᏁᏫᏔᏍᎠᎾᏗ

ᎠᎥ ᏦᏲᎵᏂᎵ ᏲᏂᏋ ᎠᏎᎠᎵ. ᎤᏲᎩᎤᏋᏫᏏ
ᎠᎥ ᎠᏫᎵ ᏍᏃᎥᎵᏪᎫ, ᎤᏲᏗ ᎠᏨ, ᎤᏁᏍ ᎠᏋ,
ᏒᎢ ᎩᏟ, ᎠᏍ ᎤᏢᏴᏬᏍ ᎯᎾ. ᏍᎵᏒᎵᏍ ᏂᎷᎷᎩ.
ᎬᏂᎫᎤᎢ.

ᎠᎥ ᎷᏋᏦ ᏮᏕᎷᏪ.

ᏝᏖᎠ ᎠᏎᎢᎵᎤ. ᏦᏆᎬᎤ ᎢᎬᎤᎵᏋᏝᎵᏂᎵ
ᎠᎯᏫᎩ.

ᏫᏝᏦ ᎤᎪᎵᏫᏝᎵᏂ ᎠᎯᏴᎤᏫ. ᎠᎥ ᎯᏍᏝ
ᎠᎯᏴᎤᏫ. ᏪᏍᏝᏋᏫᏍᏫᎵ.

ᏦᏝᎤ ᏲᏂᏋ ᎠᏎᎠᎵ

Contents

Acknowledgments

This work would not have developed beyond just an idea without the help and encouragement of my husband, our family, and our dear friend Linda Adler.

The project itself could not have taken place without all the First Nations individuals who agreed to participate. Thank you all for your insights and your willingness to voice them.

Thanks also to Raymond Farve, chair of American Indian Studies at Haskell Indian Nations University; Dr. Robert Venables of Cornell University; and the students at the Telluride House at Cornell University (where I was a Visiting Fellow), who brought a global perspective to "Indian" stereotypes and who helped me see how they perceived First Nations peoples.

Additionally, thanks to the University of Arizona's scholarly journal *Red Ink* for continuing to bring First Nations issues to academic attention.

Discussion of Terms Used

FIRST NATIONS. The use of this term for describing the Indigenous peoples of North America has had increased usage in recent years. The peoples who are indigenous to North America were here prior to the arrival of Europeans and hence are "first." As Yvonne Murry-Ramos wrote, "Each tribe has a sovereign legal status (above that of a state's in most instances), each tribe has its own customs, language, and world view. In other words, each indigenous tribe is a separate nation" (quoted in Hirschfelder, 30).

HEALER. See "medicine man."

"INDIAN." In 1990, Lenore Keeshig-Tobias said, "How I loathe the term 'Indian.' . . . 'Indian' is a term used to sell things—souvenirs, cigars, cigarettes, gasoline, cars. . . . 'Indian' is a figment of the white man's imagination," adding that "the word *Indian* merely commemorates Columbus's mistake" and is an erroneous generalization that has contributed greatly to the marginalization of First Nations peoples of North America (quoted in Wright, ix). I agree with Michael Yellow Bird that the terms "Indian," "American Indian," and "Native American" promote "oppressive, counterfeit identities" (quoted in Pewewardy, "Renaming Ourselves," 15); hence my use of quotation marks around those terms throughout this work.

"INDIAN MYSTICISM." Hollywood has transposed India Indian mysticism onto First Nations socioreligious cultures in creating "Native American" characters who possess qualities, abilities, or characteristics of "Indian mysticism." In his "quest for the ultimate reality," Ramchandra Dattatraya Ranade—"by the grace" of his guru—reached "the very core of his existence," with his guru playing "the key role in the right understanding of these divine experiences."[1]

Swami Muktananda describes an India mystic or guru as

... the master of all the primordial elements that make up the universe His words are mantras and materialize as the choicest blessings of God, the supreme reality. The world can neither understand him nor comprehend his actions. Awestruck by his greatness and his command over the elements, people call him a mystic. Nevertheless, for those who understand the subtle causal relationship between the form and the formless, the world and its creator, there is nothing enigmatic about such a being. . . . Their lives fall into a single beautiful pattern, for they are one with That which is unending bliss, That which projects the entire universe on the screen of its own Self without any external aid or material.[2]

Ranade, however, acknowledges that India Indian mysticism is often considered a signifier of "any occult or mysterious phenomena."[3] Likewise, Hollywood writers, directors, and producers lump American "Indian mysticism" into the arena of the occult, such as witnessed in the "Indian" episodes of *The X-Files*.

Similarly, First Nations and military historian Tasiwoopa ápi explains Euro-Americans' idea of "Indian mysticism" as the following:

It is an ephemeral belief system that takes certain individuals within the society and defines them and endows them with supernatural powers like the "hands-on" healers in Christian belief who are in a strata above preacher but below God. It's believed that they have a direct connection with God that gives them the supernatural powers. Whites want to try and raise First Nations healers and medicine people into this strata. We don't believe in this concept that our healers are classified as deities. It is something whites perceive as lacking in their own religions that sends them looking for so-called "Indian mystics."[4]

All too many Europeans and Euro-Americans who seek out First Nations socioreligious cultures have done so because they feel trapped in an urban/industrialized world where they had no control over their day-to-day lives or their work environment and where they even lacked the luxury of pursuing fulfillment through the arts or humanities during their free time. Europeans and Euro-Americans, especially during the nineteenth and twentieth centuries, "supposed that American Indians enjoyed real satisfactions in their daily lives, 'authentic' lives of 'genuine' culture."[5] Therefore many Europeans and Euro-Americans, as exemplified by German immigrant Adolf Gutohrlein (aka Adolf Hungry Wolf), went looking for a First Nations "Indian mystic," a "guru in a genuine [North American] Indian community."[6] But Gutohrlein endowed these Naturvölker (natural people), as he referred to them in his books, with the attributes of India Indian mystic gurus, just as Hollywood has.

Gutohrlein's Naturvölker lived away from civilized life in harmony with the natural world, where they were the keepers of "primordial wisdom that could heal our troubled world."[7] Compare this description with Ranade's discussions of India Indian mystics who follow the "philosophic reflections of the ancient seers" who "lived in cloisters far away from the bustle of humanity," where the "individual self has become one with the universal Self."[8]

"INDIAN PRINCESS."   The "Indian princess" can be defined in two ways. The first reflects the fact that the early European invaders had never witnessed any type of government structure other than monarchies. They could comprehend leaders only as kings, wives of leaders as queens, and sons and daughters as princes and princesses. Hence the daughter of an "Indian chief" had to be a princess.

Christian F. Feest offers the second explanation for the classic American "Indian princess" rooted in the "American origin myth" of Pocahontas, John Smith, and John Rolfe:

Pocahontas was made to symbolize a virginal native America, for her representation was merged with the older Indian Queen and Indian Princess images. In mystic form, by saving Smith she legitimized the Anglo-American presence in North America. By marrying Rolfe she conveys the aboriginals' title to the land to the English colonists and accepts a dependent status for native Americans. By her early death she makes room for Euroamerican expansion as all good Indians should. For Virginians there were additional dimensions: her alleged contribution to her husband's experiments with tobacco cultivation helped to establish the basis for Virginia's economic prosperity, while through her son, Thomas, she infused the blood of native American "royalty" into the veins of the colonial elite.[9]

INDIAN SPIRITUALITY.   The holistic acceptance of all facets of daily life; religion, social norms (mores), politics, education, child rearing, obtaining and preparing food, health care, elder care, matters of state, intra- and intertribal (sovereign nation to sovereign nation), conflict and mediation, and the many other aspects of daily cultural socioreligious belief systems. This intrinsic set of everyday beliefs and social norms is the antithesis of the cultural norms the American government forced on the First Nations peoples through the political policies of assimilation, which included the distribution of treaty-guaranteed food, clothing, and housing by Christian organizations that forced their distributees to attend church in order to receive their allotments. This particular activity would never occur under traditional circumstances. Religion, feeding and clothing the People, and seeing to their needs were responsibilities of the elders, the warrior societies, and the healers. Many First Nation Sovereign Nations have returned to the traditional form of consensus government in which all voices are heard and the needs of all are seen to and dealt with. In all forms of Indian Spirituality there is no separation of church and state, as they are continuously intertwined. The degradation of the First Nations belief systems by the imposition of the ideology of mysticism also has had a negative impact on the sovereign societies.

In her book *American Indians: Stereotypes and Realities*, Devon A. Mihesuah offers this definition of "Indian spirituality":

Indian spirituality is not just an oversimplified "love of nature and all living things," as some non-Indians interpret it to be. Indian spirituality permeates all aspects of life: physical, emotional and social. The various aspects of one's life, including religion, work, warfare, social activities, education, eating and playing are not compartmentalized to a daily or weekly schedule. All aspects are closely intertwined, and it is not easy to explain or understand. Indian religions tend to be only superficially understood—or totally misunderstood—by non-Indians. Each tribe has its own religious traditions, with ceremonies to mark the seasons, to give thanks, to ask for prosperous hunting and growing, in addition to specific ways to sing, dance, and to bury their dead. Like other aspects of Indians' cultures, their religions cannot be generalized.[10]

INDIGENOUS. The term "Indigenous" is used in the same way as "European," "Aboriginal," or "American" and therefore is capitalized.

MEDICINE MAN. The term "medicine man" falls into the same category as "Indian." "Medicine man"—or "medicine woman" for that matter—carries negative stereotypical connotations and is an erroneous generalization. The dominant society, thinking that it is being more politically correct, has in recent years replaced "medicine man" with "shaman." This is an even more incorrect European term, which, according to *The Random House Dictionary of the English Language*, second edition unabridged, came into usage around 1690 and is of Russian origin. In the dictionary definition, a shaman is a person among "certain tribal peoples" who "acts as intermediary between the natural and supernatural worlds, using magic to cure illness, foretell the future, control spiritual forces, etc.," and Shamanistic religions are "animistic" and embrace "a belief in powerful spirits that can be influenced only by shamans." First, every one of the more than five hundred Indigenous Nations within the United States has its own name for healers and religious leaders. Second, healers treat patients holistically with herbs, used internally and externally, and with prayers, so the treatment is "magic" only in the same sense that penicillin was considered a "magic bullet." Third, the dominant society has erroneously judged Indigenous religions of North America to be "animistic" since the days of early contact, when whites mistook ceremonies and celebrations connected *with* animals as worship *of* animals. (See the writings of James Adair, James Mooney, and Henry Schoolcraft, to name but a few.)

MEDICINE PEOPLE.   In Indigenous cultures, healers can be, and often are, women, as well as men. To lump all healers under the term "medicine man" or "shaman" is incorrect. (See "Medicine man," above.) In many First Nations, young boys and girls with a natural tendency toward healing are chosen to apprentice with a healer or a medicine society, and they spend the rest of their lives learning and teaching the healing arts.

POW WOW.   This term is spelled as "powwow" in standard dictionaries and in *O Brave New Words! Native American Loanwords in Current English*, but in *News from Indian Country*—an Indigenous-owned, -managed, and -written newspaper with subscribers in fourteen countries—spells the word "pow wow" (Cutler, 192). "Powwow" is an English corruption of "pow wa," according to Laughing Woman, a tribal elder of the Connecticut Mashantucket Pequots. She said that "pow wa is the gathering of Native Americans," while she was uncertain of any real meaning for "powwow" ("Schemitzun!").

SHAPE SHIFTER.   Shape shifters are a part of many First Nations cultures and have become popular plot devices in recent popular literature—especially the subgenre of horror/science fiction. In *Shape-shifting: Images of Native Americans in Recent Popular Fiction*, Macdonald, Macdonald, and Sheridan describe shape shifting as "a human being changing into another living creature—for example, the shamanistic idea of the Lakota Sioux warriors shape-shifting into buffalo or wolves to enhance hunting skills and to honor the animal hunted." The authors add, "In general, it carries the idea of metamorphosis, of transformation from one form to another, or to some degree, becoming the other, sharing point of view and lifeway" (xiv–xv). See their book for more information about shape shifting. For an extended study into whether shape shifting is considered literal or figurative in First Nations societies, written from a Euro-American perspective, see Calvin Luther Martin, *The Way of the Human Being* (New Haven, CT: Yale University Press, 1999).

TRADITIONAL.   To many non-Indigenous people, the term "traditional" refers to a First Nations individual who "still speaks his or her language and practices tribal religious ceremonies." However, as Mihesuah points out in *American Indians: Stereotypes and Realities*, this definition of "traditional" applies only to more recent times, for "Plains Indians who rode horses in the 1860s are considered traditional today, but were not the same as their traditional ancestors of the early 1500s who had never seen a horse" (16). In this work, "traditional" refers to First Nations individuals who practice what their individual nation considers to be the customary mores of their people (i.e., traditional culture), regardless of whether or not the individual was raised on a reservation. It's another stereotype to think that only "reservation Indians" know, understand, practice, or were raised with traditional culture or in a traditional tribal environment (Mihesuah, 16, 76–78, 108–109). Furthermore, due to the federal government's assimilation policies, many First Nations individuals do not know their native languages. This does not, however, preclude many of them from knowing or practicing their nation's customs, ceremonies, and religious beliefs.

Introduction

*Like feature films, television confined Native
Americans to a handful of tribes and cultures and then
redrafted them to suit popular conceptions. Screen
Indians belonged only to Plains tribes, spoke the same
language, dressed in the same clothes, and practiced
the same religion.*

—ANNETTE M. TAYLOR
Cultural Heritage in Northern Exposure

I remember how excited I got when the *Star Trek* episode "The Paradise Syndrome" aired because I could lose myself in the story, and, for a single hour that Friday night it was OK for me to be me, the Indigenous me.[1] It didn't matter that the "Indian" characters had as much depth as a sheet of onionskin or that the way they were represented on our new color TV reeked of inaccuracy, stupidity, and that generic jumble of which Annette M. Taylor speaks. None of that mattered. It was the only time I could remember seeing TV "Indians" who were not being chased by the cavalry or shot by cowboys and whose intent was not to massacre innocent settlers. That *Star Trek* episode had a profound affect on me as a young girl whose people were hardly mentioned in American history books in school, whose classmates were overwhelmingly white, whose way of looking at and interacting with the world was "different" from that of the other kids, and whose daily life included having to coexist with "Indian" stereotypes that had no grounding in reality but were ones the dominant society expected me to resemble because they passionately believed the stereotypes.

Euro-Americans appear not to realize that the "Indian" stereotypes they are constantly bombarded with on television *are* stereotypes rather than realistic depictions of First Nations peoples. Movie and television viewers have had a steady diet of the feathers and the fantasy for over a hundred years, through which they have learned what it supposedly means to be a "real Indian."[2]

This stereotypical life of these supposed "real Indians" depicted in movies and television is a hodgepodge of authentic items added to the filmmaker's own fantasy.[3] For example, a "Tonto-figure" or other "strange, romantic, demonic, dangerous . . . Indian as virile barbarian" (i.e., the "typical Hollywood Indian man") bursts onto the screen, wearing "a long, flowing, feathered headdress, a breech cloth . . . and moccasins" and wielding "a fierce-looking tomahawk," while his sister, "the little Indian Maiden" or "the Indian Princess," who is "maidenly, demure and deeply committed to some white man" (i.e., the typical Pocahontas), sports a long or short "beaded and fringed buckskin dress and a beaded headband with one feather sticking straight up in the back."[4] He hunts buffalo or does nothing at all, and she gathers berries and wild herbs, makes pottery and baskets, and slaves away at the buffalo hides or cooking fire outside their teepee.[5] According to the writers, directors, and producers of the entertainment seen on television, this imagery applies to nineteenth-century "Indians" as well as to modern-day twenty-first-century First Nations individuals and even to those living in the twenty-third century.

Colleagues have often asked me why I am so passionate when it comes to the stereotypical depictions of "Indians" in movies and on TV, and especially in science fiction, since I am, like several participants in this study, a fan of the genre. It is after all, as my colleagues are quick to point out, *fiction*. Unfortunately, movie and TV fiction have become accepted as America's facts (and the world's for that matter) when it comes to "Indians." My response is that I am so passionate because these careless and universally accepted stereotypes do damage. Negative "Indian" stereotypes do physical, mental, emotional, and financial harm to First Nations individuals.

My husband, who is also a First Nations individual, and I have been forced to put up with the fallout from so-called harmless "Indian" stereotypes all of our lives. We have been denied jobs for which we were overqualified, due to the stereotype that all "Indians" are lazy and drunks. Or as Andrew J. Orkin stated in explaining the dominant society's attitude toward the employment of "Indians," the stereotype that is perceived as reality is that we are "shiftless won't-works, recipients of handouts and a drain on the national economy."[6] A statement made in 1816 by Cyrus Kingsbury, the founder of the Christian mission school at Brainerd, Tennessee, aptly demonstrates the Euro-American's belief that they must assume a parental role in order "to form them ['Indians'] to habits of industry, and to give them competent knowledge of the economy of civilized life."[7]

We have also faced similar discrimination in academic and other areas. A law professor at a southeastern university once informed me that "Indians" had no place in a discussion of First Amendment rights.

I found that rather odd, given that the First Amendment deals with such items as freedom of speech, freedom of the press, and freedom of religion, but federal governmental policies and do-gooders' desires to transform "bad Indians" into "good Indians" have resulted in the denial of these First Amendment rights to First Nations individuals, even though they are U.S. citizens.[8]

Unfortunately, employment and academia rank are only two areas where stereotype-based racism applies. For example, when our home was vandalized and we reported the incident to the police, they said we were "primitive savages" and told to "go back to where you came from," as if we were the foreigners living on this continent. The root of this particular attitude dates back to Columbus's arrival in the "New World," when Europeans demonstrated that they believed they had a moral right to lay waste to the land and its people. Or as Horace Greeley so aptly expressed this attitude, "These people [First Nations individuals] must die out—there is no help for them. God has given this earth to those who will subdue and cultivate it, and it is vain to struggle against His righteous decree."[9] Greeley, as the editor of the *New York Tribune*, took the outrageous, inaccurate, and sensationalized accounts of First Nations peoples published in colonial newspapers and ran with them, greatly contributing to the perpetuation of the "barbaric," "cruel and cowardly," "stealing," "squalid and conceited, proud and worthless, lazy and lousy" "Indian" stereotypes that Hollywood latched onto and perfected—the same labeling my husband and I have had to deal with at every turn.[10]

In addition to being discriminated against in the workplace and in the academic world, we have been denied medical care because everybody assumes that "Indians" sponge off the government, so the government could take care of our medical needs.

My husband and I have also been the victims of ethnic profiling by store security and the police while shopping in a large Midwestern city, because of the stereotype of "Indians" being thieves and criminals. My husband's civil rights were denied him in a state court due to profiling activities by a county sheriff's department. Constitutional rights are nonexistent in our state court system because a number of western states refuse to acknowledge the rights of any Indigenous sovereign nation. These states still actively promote ethnic profiling based on "Indian" stereotypes in order to deny First Nations individuals their federal civil and constitutional rights. The ideology behind the derogatory term "prairie nigger," as used by officers of a state court system, is alive and well and continues to promote the negative stereotype of First Nations individuals among the dominant society and, in particular, law enforcement.

The "dumb Injin" categorization allows otherwise intelligent individuals to treat us First Nations people as if we have the IQ of mo-rons. We have been told we can't possibly know our own history. We have even been told we have no right to claim being "Indian" because we didn't study "Indians," "Indian history," and "Indian religion" in white schools. For that matter, dominant-society individuals insist that we can't possibly have "Indian religion" because "Indians" don't have the equivalent of "Sunday school" where "Indian" children can learn religion. Clinging to the "Indian" stereotypes, these non-Indigenous individuals refuse to accept that our religious education is not limited to two hours on Sunday morning or an hour on Sunday or Wednesday night. For us, religion is not restricted or compartmentalized to a par-ticular hour or a particular day. It is part of every minute of every day from the moment we are born. We live our religions.

I was writing the *Wyoming Guide* a few years after the National Park Service first included "Indian" traditions and cultural associa-tions concerning the sacredness of the site known as Bear's Lodge (dis-respectfully called Devil's Tower by Colonel Richard I. Dodge in 1875). To promote western tourism, President Theodore Roosevelt proclaimed the volcanic butte to be the first national monument in the United States in 1906, but rock climbers have been "conquering" it since 1893. Many expressed outrage that the National Park Service would even consider allowing the Lakotas the right to hold their Sun Dance each June near their sacred site. In reaction, members of the local non–First Nations population told me that "seeing as how the 'Indians' had never bothered to hold any ceremonies here in the past, why all of a sudden do they want to hold them now?" Sadly, these members of the dominant society were unaware of or ignored the fact that until and after the passage of the Native American Religious Freedom Act of 1978 (yes, *1978*), it was against federal law for First Nations people, who had been citizens of the United States since 1924 and who supposedly enjoyed all the rights and privileges of the Constitution of the United States and its amendments, to practice their religions. Despite this federal law, widespread legal persecution of First Nations individuals participating in traditional religious ceremonies such as the Sun Dance continued until the early 1990s.

Even now, many if not most non-Indigenous people have little under-standing of First Nations religions. When I asked for the time off work to attend the Sun Dance, one of my coworkers wrinkled her brow and said, "That's in Utah, isn't it? Robert Redford runs it, doesn't he?" She of course was referring to the location of the Sundance Film Festival, which Redford named after his movie portrayal of Harry Longabaugh, also known as the Sundance Kid. Other coworkers told me to "have a good time at the pow wow."

Granted, certain ceremonies conducted at pow wows are deeply significant to First Nations peoples and are very religious in nature. Pow wows, however, are social gatherings and, unfortunately, the congregation spot for racism in one of its worst forms—the anthropologist. Anthropologists, in broad terms, need not be professionals but simply those who feel they have the right to steal the images of First Nations individuals in any form at any time—the obnoxious photographers who believe they have an absolute entitlement to take anybody's picture even after the individual tells them no. As Richard Hill, a Mohawk artist, has remarked: "Nearly all Indians have been asked to 'pose' for a visitor's camera, and the visitor leaves with his personal image of 'real, live Indians.' . . . Stories about White photographers entered tribal oral histories and the camera became the latest weapon to be used against Indians. . . . The camera was an intrusion on Indian life. The photographs were taken for outside interests, by outside people, outside of the needs of Indians themselves."[11]

There was such a photographer at the pow wow my husband and I recently attended on the reservation. We had dressed to participate in the Grand Entrance Veterans' songs and flag ceremony. A photographer started to take my husband's picture without permission. When my husband told the man no pictures, the photographer tried it again from a greater distance. When that didn't work, he got his son to try to get pictures. My husband again said no. The photographer then whined to the pow wow officials. They told the photographer he could not take anyone's picture without first obtaining permission. It took my husband donning his Green Beret before the photographer finally decided it might not be wise to press the issue any further. But we still caught him trying to take First Nations children's pictures who were not participating in the pow wow dances. His attitude was that every First Nations person attending the pow wow was there on display for his entertainment and edification.

Unfortunately, children today are learning the same stereotypes as their parents did. When we give talks to grade-school children, the kids start dancing around, whooping with their hands over their mouths in classic Hollywood fashion, and greeting us with the word "How!" They want to know where we tied up our horses. They ask if we live in a teepee. They demand to know why we aren't wearing feathers. They ask to see our collection of scalps. They are shocked or surprised when we smile or laugh. And inevitably one child informs us that his or her great-great-great-granddaddy married an "Indian princess."

Such comments, questions, and prejudicial treatment are all based on the "Indian" stereotypes presented in movies and on TV. They are all stereotypes that appeared in the seven episodes reviewed by First

Nations participants for the present study, and they are all stereotypes that all First Nations individuals must deal with daily. For the most part, they let it roll off their backs and go on with their lives as best they can. Occasionally, however, when a number of blatant discriminatory remarks and bigoted actions occur in rapid succession, patience and tolerance disappear. The "angry Indian" label is not always a stereotype. It's sometimes a reaction to the stupidity, arrogance, and hatred displayed by the dominant society. Stereotypes do harm.

The majority of my husband's and my personal encounters with "Indian" stereotyping discussed here have taken place within the past few years. This is one of the reasons why the U.S. Supreme Court reaffirmed Affirmative Action in 2003. Even though we are in the twenty-first century, minorities still continue to face discrimination based on five-hundred-year-old characterizations. It may be a new millennium, but it's already filled with very old stereotypes about the Indigenous population of this country.

In 1991, Linda P. Rouse and Jeffery R. Hanson conducted a study in "Indian" stereotyping and status-based prejudices at universities in Texas, North Dakota, and Wisconsin.[12] They found that "ninety-five percent of what students know about American Indians was acquired through the media."[13] In this way the problem has been defined and observed from both an informal and an academic point of view.[14]

The purpose of this book is to explore participation responses of First Nations peoples to the "Indian" stereotypes portrayed within the TV science fiction genre, in seven representative episodes: *Star Trek* "The Paradise Syndrome," *My Favorite Martian* "Go West, Young Martian, Go West, Part II," *Star Trek: Voyager* "Tattoo," and *Quantum Leap* "Freedom," which look at general Indigenous stereotyping; and *The Adventures of Superman* "Test of a Warrior," *Star Trek: The Next Generation* "Journey's End," and *Star Trek: Voyager* "The Cloud," which examine "American Indian" religions and spirituality. It is my intent to give a voice to First Nations peoples' reactions to the stereotypes in these representative episodes.

By the same token, I have been asked, "Why science fiction?" My response is, "Why not science fiction? Are First Nations peoples supposed to be portrayed only in westerns, as the losers to the greater good of manifest destiny?" Historians, ethnographers, anthropologists, archaeologists, and the media persist in relegating First Nations peoples to the past, a tradition carried on in TV westerns. No contemporary TV genre includes First Nations characters. Furthermore, science fiction is the only genre that suggests that First Nations peoples and their cultures have a future that has not been assimilated into the dominant society. This feature of science fiction is significant to First Nations individuals. There is a great irony found within the genre. While allowing First Nations peoples to have their own cultures in the future, which in itself defies well-established "Indian" stereotypes, the writers, producers, and directors of TV science fiction constantly rely on "Indian" stereotypes in their story lines. Thus science fiction is the perfect paradox for such a study.

Furthermore, my study was not designed to be a compendium of every "Indian" episode in TV science fiction. The study looked at normal everyday "Indian" life and spirituality as depicted through the futuristic genre, which is why I purposefully did not include *The X-Files* "Indian" episodes in my study. First, *The X-Files* has had an enormous amount of dissection in print, mostly from the dominant-society perspective. Second, the show's "Indian" episodes described Hollywood's idea of "Indian" mysticism rather than spirituality (see "Discussion of Terms Used"); thus *The X-Files* episodes did not fall into the categories studied. Third, the majority of the participants were viewing the chosen episodes for the first time, whereas most of them had previously seen the *X-Files* episodes. To ensure honest evaluation of the images, there was no discussion of the episodes or shows prior to the viewing and filling out of the questionnaires.

Chapter 1 looks at the methodological approaches used in this research project, which presents the responses of First Nations peoples' perceptions of stereotyped portrayals of cultural traditions within the selected TV science fiction episodes. Thus, it examines the stereotype of "Indians" from the exclusive perspective and voices of First Nations peoples. Within-cultural-group (internal) research is needed if we are to begin to address the cognitive, social, and psychological effects that such forms of racism that stereotypes have on those who are being portrayed. The overwhelming majority of literature about "Indians"— be it history books, novels, or television scripts—is written by and from the perspective of non-Indigenous people.[15] Ward Churchill, in his book *Fantasies of the Master Race*, refers to the "the new racist intellectualism" of Euro-American authors such as James A. Clifton and Werner Sollors, who warn scholars, as a methodological approach to studying "Indians," to dismiss anything that "Indians" say:

This is to say that all work done about Indians by Indians—or by non-Indians, but with which Indians are known to agree—should, no matter what its presentation or documentation, be disregarded out of hand as "partisan . . . intellectual atrocities." "Sound scholarship" requires that all such material be (re)interpreted by "responsible" Euroamerican academics who, above all else, embody the necessary "distance" and "objectivity" necessary to arrive at "realistic" determinations about any people of color (by the same fallacy, of course, this would mean only people of color possess the neutrality and perspective needed to analyze and assess Euroamerica, but this point seems never to have dawned on either Sollors or Clifton).[16]

Yet that "distance" and "objectivity" rarely make it into scholarly works about "Indians" authored by non-Indigenous people; instead their so-called objective scholarship is, as Linda Tuhiwai Smith points out in *Decolonizing Methodologies: Research and Indigenous Peoples,* "inextricably linked to European imperialism and colonialism."[17] Smith elaborates: "Research 'through imperial eyes' describes an approach which assumes that Western ideas about the most fundamental things are the only ideas possible to hold, certainly the only rational ideas, and the only ideas which can make sense of the world, or reality, of social life and of human beings."[18] Smith's observations imply that First Nations peoples must remain absent from the picture (or the script), leaving only "cinematic stereotyping within North America's advanced colonial system."[19]

Chapter 2 deconstructs the term "stereotyping" and identifies relevant factors that underlie these particular ethnic stereotypes. The creation of a stereotype for a group of people allows another group of people to rationalize their prejudicial treatment of that group.[20] In the case of First Nations peoples, stereotyping began with the first written accounts soon after Columbus arrived, became fixed in the minds of Europeans and Euro-Americans during the colonial period through oral and written sources, and became visual perceptions with the invention of the moving camera. These centuries-old stereotypes made their way onto the small screen soon after its birth, and today are projected into approximately 80 percent of American homes via satellite or cable TV.[21] An overview of "Indians" in TV science fiction follows the discussion of stereotypes.

Chapter 3 explores science fiction television shows that aired between 1965 and 1995, using synopses and textual analyses of three shows that illustrate and challenge "Indian" stereotypes in primarily nonspiritual, day-to-day living situations. The episodes are arranged chronologically. Following this, First Nations peoples voice their reactions to and concerns about the images portrayed in these shows.

Chapter 4 offers a unique study of the *Quantum Leap* "Freedom" episode. In addition to commentary by a general cross section of First Nations individuals after viewing the depiction of Shoshone "Indian" stereotypes in the episode, a group of Shoshones critiqued Hollywood's interpretation of the everyday life of Shoshones. As in chapter 3, these discussions follow a synopsis and textual analysis of the episode.

Chapter 5 focuses on Hollywood's interpretation of "Indian" spirituality and discusses how First Nations peoples view Hollywood's efforts to portray "American Indian" spiritual traditions and practices in TV science fiction. The first portion of the chapter contains the synopsis and the textual analysis that challenges "Indian" stereotypes seen in three specific episodes from shows that aired between 1954 and 1995. These episodes, also presented chronologically, offer classic examples of formulaic "Indian" spirituality and religious practices found in science fiction TV shows. In the second portion of the chapter, First Nations peoples share their opinions of Hollywood's stereotypes of "Indian" spirituality.

Chapter 6 sums up the concerns of First Nations peoples and, using this summary as a foundation, hypothesizes how the reader can begin to view more clearly how centuries-old stereotypes continue to reinforce racial prejudices that persist to this day.

First Nations Voices on Hollywood "Indians"

*T*he Euro-American research tradition is based on Cartesian ideas related to what constitutes scientific thinking or observing that are related to the bifurcation of functions or systems.[1] Yet this long tradition, which designates itself as the group to which all others must be compared, is now understanding that some of its ideas may not be generalizable to specific groups of ethnic minorities. This belief is finally giving way to a new call for research within specific cultures by mainstream researchers for the purpose of identifying commonalities within responses of those cultures.[2] The impact of the culture in which one is raised directly relates to how the individuals from the culture relate to one another and the world. Cultures and all that encompasses work to design the formation of individuals' contents of mind, how knowledge is organized. The need for further within-culture research on individual perception of and subsequent cognitions about information presented to individuals has begun to be realized.[3]

A similar call for changes in paradigms within quantitative and qualitative research is being sounded among Indigenous voices. Linda Tuhiwai Smith has stated that Indigenous research is "inextricably linked to European imperialism and colonialism."[4] Silencing Indigenous voices is part of this long heritage of European imperialism and colonialism, as Smith explains:

It galls us that Western researchers and intellectuals can assume to know all that it is possible to know of us, on the basis of their brief encounters with some of us. It appalls us that the West can desire, extract and claim ownership of our ways of knowing, our imagery, the things we create and produce, and then simultaneously reject the people who created and developed those ideas and seek to deny them further opportunities to be creators of their own culture and own nations.[5]

The primary purpose of this research project was to address the responses of First Nations adults' perceptions of the portrayal of cultural traditions and stereotypes of "American Indians" within a selected set of videotaped clips. For all of the reasons given above, only First Nations peoples participated in this research. Participants responded to structured surveys in a large group.

Selection of Participants

Participants in the groups represent a diverse Indigenous population representing several highly differentiated nations, each with distinct spiritual beliefs. Participants ranged in age from 18 to 55, with a mean age of 26. All are members of federally recognized members of First Nations.

Participants who discussed their tribal affiliation and/or spiritual beliefs did so strictly on a voluntary basis. Additionally, participants were given the option to classify themselves as science fiction fans. Fourteen voluntarily admitted that they were fans of the genre and of the *Star Trek* sagas in particular.

Selection of all participants was on a convenience group basis.

Survey Group 1
Seventeen women and 12 men between the ages of 18 to 55, with a mean age of 26, participated in the first focus group. They came from federal recognized Indigenous nations from the Midwest and the western sections of the United States and Alaska.

Survey Group 2
Thirteen women and 5 men between the ages of 21 to 50, with a mean age of 28, participated in the second focus group. They came from federal recognized Indigenous nations from across the continental United States.

Shoshone Survey Groups
Seven women and three men between the ages of 18 and 46, with a mean age of 22, participated in the all-Shoshone focus groups. All came from branches of the Shoshone Nation that are federally recognized.

Videotaped Clips

All of the science fiction episodes used in all groups are part of the author's personal collection, taped from television between 1990 and 2001. In each of the surveys, the clips were arranged in chronological order for viewing (see table 1.1).

Each of the clips was examined by participants in order to understand the effect of and common threads among responses to stereotypes

Table 1.1 **TV Episodes Viewed by Each Survey Group**

Group	Survey	TV episodes viewed
Survey Group 1	Stereotyping Indigenous peoples in science fiction TV shows	*My Favorite Martian* "Go West, Young Martian, Go West, Part II" (1965) *Star Trek* "The Paradise Syndrome" (1968) *Quantum Leap* "Freedom" (1990) *Star Trek: Voyager* "Tattoo" (1995)
Survey Group 2	"American Indian" religions and spirituality stereotyping in science fiction TV shows	*The Adventures of Superman* "Test of a Warrior" (1954) *Star Trek: The Next Generation* "Journey's End" (1994) *Star Trek: Voyager* "The Cloud" (1995)
Shoshone Survey Group	Stereotyping Shoshones in the science fiction TV show *Quantum Leap*	*Quantum Leap* "Freedom" (1990)

within the clips. Clips were selected to portray possible examples of the most common and pervasive "Indian" stereotypes currently shown on television. In Survey Group 1, four clips were chosen that depict general "Indian" lifeways and customs: *My Favorite Martian* "Go West, Young Martian, Go West, Part II"; *Star Trek* "The Paradise Syndrome"; *Quantum Leap* "Freedom"; and *Star Trek: Voyager* "Tattoo." A synopsis and textual analysis of the episodes viewed for Survey 1, arranged chronologically, with the exception of *Quantum Leap*, as well as the First Nations peoples' concerns raised in the survey will be discussed in chapter 3. The synopsis and textual analysis of the *Quantum Leap* "Freedom" episode and the commentary of the First Nations individuals from Survey Group 1 and from the Shoshone Survey Groups will be explored in chapter 4. In Survey Group 2, *The Adventures of Superman* episode "Test of a Warrior," *Star Trek: The Next Generation* "Journey's End," and *Star Trek: Voyager* "The Cloud" depict aspects of "Indian" spirituality. A synopsis and textual analysis of the episodes viewed for Survey 2, arranged chronologically, as well as the First Nations peoples' concerns raised in the survey, will be discussed in chapter 5.

Survey 1

Seventeen women and 12 men saw the episodes discussed in chapter 3 in the spring of 2001 and answered the questions found in appendix A. These participants responded to the survey following the discussion after the videotaped clips were viewed.

The survey was constructed by developing a structured interview that was able to be used as a paper-and-pencil survey (appendix A). Questions were designed to be open-ended or non-leading, so that participants were free to write about their own experiences and lives rather than to attempt to read the researchers' goals by reviewing the questions. This survey was given to participants at the beginning of the video clips viewing session. No additional directions were given to the recipients of the survey. Participants had up to two weeks to return the survey after watching the video clips. They will be referred to only by number when quoted.

Survey 2

Thirteen women and 5 men saw the episodes discussed in chapter 4 in the spring of 2001 and answered the questions found in appendix C. These participants responded to the survey following the discussion after the videotaped clips were viewed.

The survey was constructed by developing a structured interview that was able to be used as a paper and pencil survey (appendix C). Questions were designed to be open-ended or non-leading so that participants were free to write about their own experiences and lives rather than to attempt to read the researchers' goals by reviewing the questions. This survey was given to participants at the beginning of the video clips viewing session. No additional directions were given to the recipients of the survey. Participants filled out and returned the survey immediately after watching the video clips. They too will only be referred to by number when quoted.

Shoshone Survey Groups

In May and June of 2001, ten Shoshones watched the *Quantum Leap* "Freedom" episode. The 7 women and 3 men ranged in age from 18 to 46, with an average age of 22. Four volunteered that they were science fiction fans. As with Survey Groups 1 and 2, the Shoshones answered the questions found in appendix B. These participants responded to the survey following the discussion after the video tape was viewed.

The survey was constructed by developing a structured interview that was able to be used as a paper and pencil survey (appendix B). Questions were designed to be open-ended or non-leading so that participants were free to write about their own experiences and lives and rather than to attempt to read the researchers' goals by reviewing the questions. This survey was given to participants at the beginning of the video clips viewing session. No additional directions were given to the recipients of the survey. Participants filled out and returned the survey immediately after watching the videotape. They too will be referred to only by number when being quoted.

Interviews of First Nations Individuals

In the fall of 2000, 7 First Nations peoples, 6 women and 1 man, responded to two questions (appendix D). The 7 Indigenous individuals interviewed are students or faculty members from universities in the western portion of the United States. They, too, will be referred to only by number when being quoted.

Summary of Methodological Strengths and Weaknesses

One strength of this methodological approach is in the sense of anonymity provided by the surveys. Although there were no focus groups associated with the surveys, casual comments/reactions to the videos, as well as participants' unconscious reactions while viewing the clips, were noted during video viewing sessions for all three surveys.

As no specific responses were being sought, other than perceptions of stereotypes, the questions were intentionally designed to be rather vague and undirected. This allowed participants total freedom in their response to the surveys. They could and did come up with unexpected and unique ways of looking at the stereotypical images of "Hollywood Indians" and Hollywood's ideas about First Nations cultures, traditions, customs, and religious beliefs. The real strength, however, lies in the fact that these are all Indigenous voices that have not been "balanced" by the dominant society's beliefs, ideas, and fantasies of "Indians."

CHAPTER 2

It's All in the Label

*F*irst Nations peoples live with stereotyping every day of their lives. A perfect example of this comes straight out of history books that Hollywood picked up on from day one. When America's educational system does include "Native American" history, it breezes through Pocahontas, Sacajawea, and the Trail of Tears and on to the *real* "Indians" who were defeated during the "Indian Wars" of the late 1870s. By focusing on the nomadic and warrior traditions of the Great Plains Nations, textbooks used in American schools have perpetuated "Indian" stereotypes that cause everybody to imagine teepees, feather bonnets, trade beads, fringed buckskin clothing, and painted pony warriors with deep copper-colored skin and long, black braids every time they see the words "Native American." The comment "Gee, you don't look like an Indian" arises from this stereotyping so faithfully followed by Hollywood today.

First Nations author Drew Hayden Taylor got so tired of hearing this comment that he wrote a book about it, titled *Funny, You Don't Look Like One: Observations from a Blue-Eyed Ojibway.* He notes, "It wasn't until I left the reserve for the big bad city, that I became more aware of the role people expected me to play, and the fact that physically, I didn't fit in. Everybody seemed to have this preconceived idea of how every Indian looked and acted." [1]

Furthermore, Carol Cornelius reports that "studies show that ninety-five percent of what students know about American Indians was acquired through the media." [2] This presents a disturbing picture when various forms of the media are examined for how they portray First Nations peoples. Hollywood, of course, picked up the "Indian Wars" era of "American history" and ran with it, typecasting the "Plains Indian" image onto movie and television screens as *the* "Indian" not only of the twentieth century but also of the twenty-fourth century.

This generic concept that "Plains Indian" equals "Native American" is also the stereotype that has helped spawn the majority of the other "Indian" stereotypes. Yet neither Hollywood nor textbooks written since the 1870s invented these "Indian" stereotypes. They just continue them, lifting them from the pages of books, magazines, and newspapers that have propagated "Indian" stereotypes since the day Christopher Columbus "discovered" *los indios* of the Americas, not the East Indies.[3]

The Label Begins

In 1958, in a book called *The Nature of Prejudice,* Gordon Allport defined stereotypes as "favorable or unfavorable [images] . . . an exaggerated belief associated with a category . . . [whose] function [it] is to justify (rationalize) our conduct in relation to that category."[4] In 1973, John C. Brigham characterized such ethnic stereotypes as "generalization, concerning trait attributions, made about the members of an ethnic group." He added, "As these [trait attributions] which recur in most discussions of stereotypes refer to their undesirable nature—a stereotype is usually seen as a generalization which is, in some sense, undesirable."[5] Brigham also pinpointed what several researchers have classified as decisive factors that underlie stereotypes:

[Stereotypes] are factually incorrect; they are products of a "faulty" or illogical thought process; they are characterized by inordinate rigidity; they are derived from an inadequate basis of acquisition, such as hearsay; they are consensual beliefs within a culture, perhaps implying a lack of individual thought; they serve a rationalization function for ethnic prejudice; they ascribe to racial inheritance that which may be cultural acquisition and they serve as justifications for prejudicial or discriminatory social practices.[6]

When these prejudicial stereotypes are applied to First Nations peoples of North America, what is "authentically Indian" becomes submerged and dehumanized by the "colonial mind set," which promotes a "falsely superior [Anglo-American] 'we' versus [Indigenous] 'them' perspective."[7] According to Cornel Pewewardy, "The colonizer's falsified stories have become universal truths to mainstream society and have reduced indigenous culture to a cartoon caricature. This distorted and manufactured reality is one of the most powerful shackles subjecting Indigenous Peoples. It distorts all indigenous experiences, past and present."[8] The result is miscommunication, misunderstanding, and "dysconscious racism," a term for a type of racism that "unconsciously accepts dominant white norms and privileges."[9] Joyce E. King elaborates: "Dysconscious racism is an uncritical habit of mind (that is, perceptions, attitudes, assumptions and beliefs) that justifies inequity and exploitation by accepting the existing order of things as given. It involves identification with an ideological view point which admits no fundamentally alternative vision of society." [10] Peter Berger and Thomas Luckmann state in their 1967 book, *The Social Construction of Reality*, "He who has the bigger stick has the better chance of imposing his definition of reality." [11] As was discussed in the introduction to the present book, writers, directors, and producers of television shows are primarily Euro-Americans who wield highly influential and enormous sticks.

The Collective "Indian"

European writers were uncertain of the identities of Indians relative to European culture, but they were clear about one point: they knew who the Indian was not. The Indian was not the European, and in many historical writings and in popular thought of the time the Indian is widely treated as an "other." [Robert] Berkhofer records a history of attempts to locate the Indian in that context through centuries of European and Euro-American images created of the Indian which were intended to strengthen an identity of the Euro-American as the representative of civilization, progress, and the future.

—CHIEF OREN LYONS AND JOHN MOHAWK,
introduction to *Exiled in
the Land of the Free*

American and world history books from the sixteenth through much of the twentieth century categorized First Nations peoples as the completely generic "Indian" to be isolated, absorbed, displaced, or conquered and vanquished. Volume 7 of the *History of the World*, discussing the rise of civilization of the United States and Great Britain, was published in 1901. The following text from that work serves as an example of the amalgamation of "Indians" in what is currently the northeast portion of the United States:

Certain tracts were also reserved by the Red men, amounting in the aggregate to about three hundred thousand acres. The theory of the [U.S.] Government was that in course of time the Indians, living on their reservations and surrounded by vast and progressive settlements of White men, would be assimilated to civilized life, and gradually absorbed as a part of the nation. It was not long, however, until it was discovered that the Indians had little sympathy with American farms and villages and American methods of life. The habits of barbarism were too strongly fixed, through ages of heredity, and no aptitude for the anticipated change was seen on the part of the sequestered aborigines.[12]

Of course, these same generic "Indians" who supposedly did not like farming were the very same ones who taught the colonists farming techniques that ensured the colonies' survival in the "New World."

Nevertheless, treating the First Nations peoples of North America as one communal group, "Indians," immediately allowed Europeans and Euro-Americans to negate the variation in First Nations societies. This need to minimize differences among the First Nations arises from the need for "simplified understanding."[13] It led to a discourse that "reinforced a language of difference that marked Indians as distinct from Europeans" in negative terms when it served the "civilized" public good.[14]

Furthermore, this consolidation of dissimilar cultures in the colonial forms of print and oral rendition led to an amalgamation of customs and traditions in readers' minds. The colonial citizen was led to the picture of all First Nations peoples of the Americas as "infidels" and "heathens" who practiced such "bestial" and "barbarous institutions" as "worship of the Devil with its emphasis on human sacrifice" or cannibalism.[15] Even the supposedly more enlightened times of the mid-1700s saw accounts such as the following one, from the August 1745 issue of *The American Magazine:* "The Indians cut open Capt. Donahew's Breast, and suck'd his Blood, & hack'd and mangled his Body in a most inhuman and barbarous Manner, and then eat a great Part of his Flesh. They also suck'd the Blood and mangled the Bodies of the other Slain, after which they carried their Prisoners to Menis, where they were about to kill and eat Mr. Picket, but he being acquainted with some of the French Inhabitants, they so far stood his Friend, (with the Assistance of the Priest) as to procure his Liberty for a Sum of Money."[16]

Articles such as this heightened British and American racism against the First Nations peoples. By dehumanizing the indigenous population of North America, by portraying them as barbarians and cannibals, politicians of the time allowed the "godly people" of Europe to justify their invasion of the New-to-them World, as well as the torture, murder, and enslavement of its inhabitants.[17] This type of racial classification thus released so-called culturally enlightened societies from having to treat the "barbarians" in a "civilized" manner, as is seen in an unofficial account of the 1838 capture of Osceola that made its way into the *Army and Navy Chronicle:* "However revolting the violation of a flag of truce may at first appear, yet when we reflect that the General [Jesup] was dealing with savages, who had once forfeited their plighted faith, and deceived him—that the interview was sought by them, and probably with the worst of motives—it is believed that he will not only be justified by public opinion, on the expediency of the measure, but will be commended for it.[18] The author's suggestion that the general was only doing what Osceola would have done, had he been given the chance, demonstrates racist attitudes that had been expressed in writing for centuries. As Robert B. Moore and Arlene B. Hirschfelder have pointed out, "The ideology of racism against Native Americans developed in colonial times to justify the physical destruction of Native peoples and nations, in order for Europeans to take over their [First Nations peoples'] lands. The ideology was later refined to justify the genocidal policies and the treaty abrogations of the U.S. as land continued to be taken away."[19]

Newspapers and magazines quickly took advantage of the need to "justify genocidal policies," running melodramatic and incendiary reports about First Nations peoples that were geared toward selling copies and subscriptions—not unlike newspapers and magazines today.[20] Additionally, sensationalism generated an increased level of fear among whites, as evidenced in a report in the 23 March 1833 issue of *The Southern Banner*. The report presented, as fact, a detailed account of the murder of a Georgia man and his family by "Indians" six months before "George Tooke," one of the "Indians" implicated in the murder and the only suspect in custody, was scheduled to be brought to trial:

The Indians killed Bowman, his mother-in-law, his wife and child, who composed every member of the family; after killing them with their usual barbarity, they split open each head with an axe, took out all they found in the house, and then set it on fire. The plundered property was sent off, by one Indian, called Creek Ben, into the Creek nation to sell. Tooke's accomplices in this murder and arson, have not yet been fully ascertained. . . .

The circumstances of this cruel outrage, we know have been variously stated and the number of persons, its victims, much augmented. Persons at a distance are, we think unnecessarily alarmed for the safety of their friends, residing in or visiting this section of the State.[21]

This report must be juxtaposed against the fact that, in direct violation of U.S. treaties signed with the Cherokees and ratified by the state of Georgia, the Georgia Legislature implemented in 1828 resolutions it had passed the year before that annexed that portion of the Cherokee Nation that the state of Georgia considered within its chartered limits and then illegally imposed Georgia laws and authority over the Cherokee people.

Also in 1828, gold was discovered in the Cherokee Nation, and whites wanted it. Georgia declared all Cherokee laws and jurisdiction null and void and put Cherokee land up for public lottery in 160-acre lots and gold lots of 40 acres. On 3 March 1832 the U.S. Supreme Court ruled that Georgia's actions were unconstitutional, but that didn't stop Georgia citizens from illegally moving into the Cherokee Nation, destroying Cherokee property, and killing Cherokees.[22] This puts a different spin on the "facts" of the 1833 *Southern Banner* article mentioned above.

Furthermore, imbedded in this colonial-era imagery that lumps all First Nations peoples together into a single "Indian" tribe are the origins of the "homogenized Indians."[23] Currently, this collective of "all-purpose Hollywood Indians" as portrayed on television actually consists of the 711 distinct First Nations that have survived to the present-day in what is now the United States.[24]

Origins of the Good, the Bad, and the Ugly "Indian" Stereotypes

By 1690 there was a distinct dichotomy in the way the press treated the First Nations peoples of North America. There were good Indians who were on their way to becoming "civilized" and bad ones who were bent on keeping their "pagan," "warlike" ways. The *Publick Occurrences* reported that year that "Christianized *Indians*" around Plymouth, thanks to "God for his Mercy," were enjoying a good harvest of corn, while "barbarous *Indians* were lurking about *Chelmsford*," where two children "belonging to a man of that Town" had disappeared three weeks previously and were "supposed to be fallen into the hands of the *Indians*."[25] This kind of view of the activity taken by "skulking" "Indians" can be traced back to Mary Rowlandson's 1673 captivity narrative that became a colonial best-seller with more than sixty print runs.

Rowlandson, the wife of a Puritan minister, and several other women and children were seized by the Wampanoags after the Massachusetts Bay Colony decided to wage war on "the Indians" in what became known at the King Philip's War (1675–1676).[26] At the time of Rowlandson's capture, the Wampanoags were fleeing the British and were taking and ransoming hostages for supplies, for the British were not only killing "the Indians" but also burning their cornfields and villages to the ground—and those of every other First Nations village that the colonists came across, a tactic that would continue in later "Indian" wars.[27] In her narrative, Rowlandson called the Wampanoags "a company of barbarous heathen."[28] Ironically, it was the very same "barbarous heathen" Wampanoags who had helped this same group of Puritans survive in 1621 and, in the process, started the tradition that became an American national holiday—Thanksgiving.[29]

As more Europeans arrived, wanting more of the First Nations peoples' land and resources, they also brought a sense of mother-country nationalism with them that incited the Europeans to war with each other on North America soil and to drag the First Nations peoples into the Europeans' squabbles. This was especially true for the British colonists, who wanted the Natives' land, as well as a corner on the European fur trade in North America.[30]

As a result, the line between friendly "Indian" and foe often blurred as English colonists fought the enemies of Great Britain and its First Nations allies. This was justified in the press with statements such as this one in *The American Museum, or Repository:* "But all savages [regardless of their being considered allies or enemies] are so much alike, they have so little hold of variation in their simple state of life, that the manners and appearance of different nations oppose no prejudices, and shock no delicacies."[31]

By the 1740s, dichotomization and racial stereotyping of the "Noble Redman" versus the "savage," the "brutal, tomahawk-wielding collector of scalps" who lives for warfare, grew even more distinct.[32] The British and colonial presses depicted the North American "savages" as noble when they paved the way for the settlers' survival and therefore for the colonies' continued existence in the "New World." The eleven- or twelve-year-old Matoaka,[33] known by her nickname or public name of Pocahontas,[34] remains the classic example of this "good-Indian-because-she-helps-whites"[35] vision, as is illustrated in a 1755 *London Magazine* article: "Pocahontas easily prevailed with her father and her countrymen to allow her to indulge her passion for the captain [John Smith], by often visiting the fort, and always accompanying her visits with a fresh supply of provisions; therefore it may justly be said, that the success of our first settlement in America, was chiefly owing to the love this young girl had conceived for Capt. Smith."[36]

Additionally, "savages" proved their "notable Warriour" valor when England needed allies to aid in its power plays over territorial rights in the "New World." A 1744 *American Magazine* article on the Six Nations of the Haudenosaunee described the First Nations people as having "strong Traces of good Sense, a nice Address in the Conduct of their Affairs, a noble Simplicity, and that manly Fortitude which is the constant Companion of Integrity" and stated that "the Honour of the Six Nations and the experienced good Intentions and Probity of the English, have been a sufficient Barrier against all their [French] Intrigues."[37]

Nevertheless, this same article illustrated the "terrible" nature of the North American "savage." The unnamed author, in the same paragraph that praised the "integrity" of the Haudenosaunees, described them as a nation "under the Appellation of Savages or Barbarians" and followed that statement with a quote from a French historian who classified Haudenosaunees as "Barbarians, always thirsting after human blood."[38]

During the Seven Years War—the politically correct term for what has been, until recently, referred to as the French and Indian War of 1754–1763—the press began to promote an "us and them" attitude that helped pull Europeans together as members of the white race, even in the midst of being at war with each other; to set them apart from all "Indians" in North America; and to give the Europeans a sense of superiority over "Indian" "inferiors."[39] The August 1760 issue of *The British Magazine, or Monthly Repository for Gentlemen and Ladies* offers a typical example:

As soon as the Indians had seized the Captain they began to strip him, which they did all to his breeches, and were carrying him off to butcher him, when a French grenadier came up, who with great difficulty (after making use of his arms and bayonet) prevented the putting their bloody design in execution, till a party of French soldiers came and rescued him out of their hand. As soon as the Captain was relieved, he offered his purse, wherein were ten guineas, which he had in his breeches pocket, to the grenadier for his behaviour, who generously refused the reward, thinking himself happy in relieving a gentleman, tho' an enemy, when in the hands of such cruel savages.[40]

At the time this article was written, the British and French had been at war for six years in the fourth conflict that pitted Old World rivals against each other in the "New World."[41] The article exemplifies the media-generated concept of "the other" to justify European infiltration and domination of the "New World."[42] Although "an enemy," the French officer considered that he had "done no more than his duty" by rescuing the British officer from the "savages," who happened to be allies of the French.[43]

The British soldiers and colonists in Virginia and South Carolina during the Seven Years War viewed their Indigenous allies no better than the French saw their "Indian" allies, and the British treated their "Indians" worse.[44] The Mohawks, one of the Six Nations in the Haudenosaunee Confederacy, gave the British their first victory in the Northeast at the Battle of Lake George in 1755; however, *The British Magazine, or Monthly Repository for Gentlemen and Ladies*, in a conversation-style article popular in the 1700s, portrayed a Mohawk man as a "North-American Savage." The English duelist in the article had never seen "one of that *species* before" and was "curious to know what the animal is."[45] The Mohawk said that he "took up the hatchet for them [the British] with the rest of my tribe in the war against

France," where he "scalped seven men and five women and children."[46] When the Englishman expressed an inability to "understand cutting the throats of women and children," the "savage" replied that it was his people's customary "way of making war."[47] Later, the Englishman turned the conversation to dining, to which the "savage" replied: *"Eat! Did you ever eat the chine of a Frenchman, or his leg, or his shoulder? There is fine eating! I have eat twenty.—My table was always well served.* My wife was the best cook for the dressing of man's flesh in all North America."[48] Once again, the "savage" was an expedient ally in war, but not one to be treated as an equal or even a human.[49]

In a more serious manner of reporting, the same magazine's Domestic Intelligence section offered great detail of British troops who "marched to the middle settlements" in the heart of their Cherokee allies' country "in good spirits, and eager for an opportunity to humble our savage enemies."[50] Although the Cherokees had been allies of the British for generations, the British saw their Cherokee allies as "enemies" because the Cherokees had been forced to defend themselves from the very British troops the Cherokees had fought alongside.[51] During the Seven Years War, the British stole Cherokee property and provisions, raped Cherokee women, and sold Cherokees into slavery.[52] Such British atrocities were not mentioned in the press, which reported only such particulars as the following: "the Indians" refused to "agree to terms of peace"; the British were "attacked within five miles of Etchoee [the Cherokees' ancient capital, although misspelled], in very advantageous ground for the enemy, by 500 Indians, which continued four or five hours"; and although "no Indians had been seen or heard of since they were beaten," the good citizens of "South-Carolina were under great apprehensions that the Indians would over-run their country without a number of regulars [British troops]" stationed there to defend the settlers.[53]

After the colonists broke with Great Britain, the citizens of the newly formed United States continued to use the "noble" and "barbarian" images of "Indians" as suited the occasion. As John M. Coward put it while researching his book *The Newspaper Indian: Native American Identity in the Press, 1820–90,* "Indians were needed in both positive and negative roles. When we needed an authentic American identity to distinguish ourselves from Europe, we embraced the romantic ideal of the Noble Savage. When we needed an enemy to vanquish in our conquest of the continent, we embraced the savage Indian as a national villain."[54]

During the second decade of the existence of the United States, the young nation's chroniclers spent a fair amount of ink on the white perspective toward the customs of the First Nations peoples. In 1789

The American Museum, or Repository carried an article on the war practices of the "American savages" who "engaged in perpetual hostilities, that are conducted with an atrocious ferocity, and unrelenting vengeance," the like of which "matured and humanized" societies could never comprehend.[55] Yet the "matured and humanized" Americans thought it was perfectly all right to offer a bounty on scalps and even participated in scalping themselves; to sell "Indian" allies, as well as enemies, into slavery; to take Osceola under a flag of truce; to allow Osceola's attending physician to cut off Osceola's head postmortem and use it to frighten his children into behaving—all in what James Axtell defended as "only a necessary adaptation of Indian means to English [and American] ends, of 'savage' tactics to 'civilized' (and therefore ultimately 'redeeming') strategies, the most important of which was the elimination of the 'Indian menace' on the ever-elastic" frontier.[56]

There was, however, a dissenting voice in the wilderness of the new nation, one willing to show the dominant society who the true "menace" was. Centuries before Ronald Takaki's *A Different Mirror: A History of Multicultural America* was written in 1993,[57] Benjamin Franklin used subtle sarcasm to hold up his own mirror to white Christian society to expose its weak spots. In the April 1789 issue of *The American Museum, or Repository,* Franklin's article "Remarks on the North American Indians" described how, after politely and attentively listening to the sermon of a Swedish minister, the leaders of the "Susquehannah Indians" proceeded to return the favor and told the minister how the people came to be given corn, kidney beans, and tobacco by the Creator. Franklin continued the story: "The good missionary, disgusted with this idle tale, said, 'what I delivered to you were sacred truths; but what you tell me is mere fable, fiction, and falsehood.' The Indian, offended, replied, 'my brother, it seems your friends have not done you justice in your education; they have not well instructed you in the rules of common civility. You saw that we, who understand and practice these rules, believed all your stories; why do you refuse to believe ours?'"[58]

In 1789, when Franklin's article appeared, Christianity was experiencing a crisis on both sides of the Atlantic after years of fighting over religious politics, propaganda against advances in science that contradicted church doctrine, rigid rituals, intolerance, and the secularization of politics.[59] Franklin's scorn of Christianity was a direct influence of the Enlightenment, begun in Europe, and of the practice of Deism, spawned out of Enlightened philosophy. Deists such as Franklin believed that "the light of knowledge" would strip away the "mysteries, miracles, and secrets" practiced by the Christians and expose the truth.[60] Franklin relished turning Deist truth on America's Christians in order to illustrate their prejudicial perspective of the First Nations peoples, driving his point home in the conclusion of his story: "You know our practice; if a white man, in traveling through our country, enters one of our cabins, we all treat him as I treat you; we dry him if he is wet, we warm him if he is cold, and give him meat and drink, that he may allay his thirst and hunger; and we spread soft furs for him to rest and sleep on; we demand nothing in return. But if I go into a white man's house at Albany, and ask for victuals and drink, they say, 'Where is your money?' and if I have none, they say, 'get out, you Indian dog.'"[61]

That same year *The American Museum, or Repository* ran an article by the Society for Propagating the Gospel among the Indians and Others in North America. According to the author, the group's sole purpose in "emigrating to this land, was professedly to extend the knowledge of our glorious Redeemer among the savage natives," as well as to "prove to the European world, who are at a great expence in pursuing this object among us, that we were not inattentive to it," and therefore they "humbly request" money from both governmental houses of the state of Massachusetts for stepping up American efforts to convert "the savages."[62]

Hollywood Picks Up the Stereotypes

Euro-Americans' efforts to categorize "Indians" into the something "noble" or something "heathen" and "warlike" spawned dichotomization that Hollywood turned into friction on the silver screen. On the side of the potentially "good Indian," the "Noble Savage" stereotype produced those "exotic but primitive creatures who might be 'saved,'" provided that "enough civilization and Christianity could be applied."[63] The image of the "sensitive, proud, peaceful children of the forest" also comes from this early depiction.[64] As such, these "children of nature" can and do "commune" with Mother Earth, thus learning and understanding all her secrets.[65] Rayna Green explains how the "Noble Savage" reaches the status of the "good Indian":

The good Indian "acts as a friend to the white man, offering ... aid, rescue, and spiritual and physical comfort even at the cost of his own life or status and comfort in his own tribe to do so. He saves white men from 'bad' Indians, and thus becomes a 'good' Indian. ... '[G]ood Indians' also lose their subjectivity, becoming part of the White person's story."[66]

The "redskinned redeemer," the "annoyingly stereotypical" "wise, saintly chief," the "mystic and mysterious" "Indian," and the 1980s–

1990s "Natural Ecologists" stereotypes have also evolved from the "Noble Savage" stereotype.[67]

Opposite the "Noble Savage" is the "Ignoble Savage" or "bloodthirsty savage" described, for example, in the 1760 account in *The British Magazine* discussed above.[68] In his quest for blood vengeance, the "Ignoble Savage" is an "infidel" "heathen" who is "treacherous," "backward," "hostile," and "utterly incompetent to cope in any way with the European or Caucasian race."[69] In this "imperialist discourse," the "Indian" becomes the "Native Other" over whom the European and Euro-American settlers must gain "psychic as well as physical control."[70] From this stereotype has evolved the "inferior," "uneducated," no-good "thieving," "Savage Sinner" "Indians" who "had no civilization until Europeans brought it to them" and "had nothing to contribute to Europeans or to the growth of America."[71] It was to this group, in order to turn them into the "Noble Savage" or even into the "good Indians," that "civilized" society became the stereotypical "white savior."[72]

With the invention of movies and television, real First Nations peoples have been "displaced by the Hollywood Indian, a cinematic creation springing directly from the ubiquitous images of the old bloodthirsty savage and his alter ego, the noble savage."[73] Ward Churchill elaborates on this: "There is no cinematic recognition whatsoever of a white-free and autonomous native past. Similarly, no attention is paid at all to the myriad indigenous nations not heavily and dramatically involved in the final period of Anglo-Indian warfare. . . . Small wonder the public views the native as some briefly extant, mythic and usually hostile apparition."[74] And Annette Taylor describes the impact of television: "Thus, television for the most part has eliminated distinctions among real Native American peoples and cultures in both the lower forty-eight states and Alaska. The overall message, whether in a turn-of-the-century or a modern-day setting, is that Indians who retain cultural identity are doomed and assimilated Indians always abandon their people."[75]

Furthermore, there is also the "Indian" perceived as the natural alien in science fiction:[76]

Embedded in every alien story is the seed of a Native American story. Just as Indians were perceived as monstrous savages, so aliens may be monstrous and savage beyond human experience: ripping, tearing, cannibalizing. And just as Indians assisted settlers and made them welcome, so some aliens are drawn as welcoming and kindly ETs, odd by mainstream standards but somehow benign. . . . The same type of embedding occurs in stories of alien fighters/warriors, alien contact for trade, alien magicians/shamans, alien romances ("I fell in love with an alien"/"I fell in love with an Indian"), and alien ecologists (with the stoic red man shedding a tear for raped Mother Earth from his spaceship, miles above).[77]

Overview of "Indian" Stereotypes in TV Science Fiction

Although westerns gave birth to the TV "Indian" in the 1950s, television also began projecting centuries-old "Indian" stereotypes into futuristic settings or, as in the episode "Test of a Warrior" of *The Adventures of Superman* (1951–1957), placing a fantasy of "Indians" still living in the "romantic" past in the midst of a contemporary setting with a humanoid space alien.[78] Hollywood, however, also reversed this situation in the 1960s by having space aliens known as "the Preservers" relocate a group of "American Indians" to a distant planet so that the latter could maintain their simple, idyllic, "noble savage" ways—in the episode "The Paradise Syndrome" of the original *Star Trek* (1966–1969). In the 1970s and much of the 1980s, both science fiction and "Indians" disappeared from the nightly TV horizon. Then the series *Quantum Leap* (1989–1993) came to the small screen, "focusing on people, rather than on the sci-fi elements of time travel."[79] Similar to *The Adventures of Superman*, *Quantum Leap* featured an "Indian" episode entitled "Freedom," which was set in a time contemporary to 1970.[80]

"Indians" also moved back to the future in the 1990s in sequels to the original *Star Trek*. "Journey's End," the "Indian" episode in *Star Trek: The Next Generation* (1987–1994) aired during the last season of the series.[81] But "Indians" didn't enter the TV science fiction mainstream until the premier of the fourth series in the *Star Trek* group, *Star Trek: Voyager* (1995–2001), which featured a "Native American" crew member with mysterious spiritual powers that came in handy from time to time.

Each of these episodes has two things in common. Each contains elements of science fiction revolving around a plotline that involves "Indian" characters, and each incorporates centuries-old stereotypes of First Nations peoples. In this manner, television has promoted "homogenize[d] perspectives, knowledge, tastes, and desires to make them resemble the tastes and interests of the people who transmit the imagery"—in this instance, members of the dominant white society.[82] Since the inception of movies and television, Hollywood (and dominant-society TV viewers) have ignored who First Nations peoples truly are and thus have effectively eliminated the possibility that "Indians" have to something to say about the way "Indians" are depicted on TV.

CHAPTER 3

Future "Indians," Past Stereotypes

> *"Native Americans in science fiction? Absurd!" Such is the likely reaction of many readers, for the conventional concept of the Indian is often fixed in the context of the historical westward movement: one way of life yielding to another just as one age gives way to the next. In fact, however, from the point of view of immigrating peoples, contact with American Indians from earliest times was an unsettling experience with the alien, the "Other." The reverse was also true.*
>
> —ANDREW MACDONALD, GINA MACDONALD,
> AND MARY ANN SHERIDAN,
> *Shape-shifting: Images of Native
> Americans in Recent Popular Fiction*

*I*n science fiction shows, the aliens who encounter and/ or interact with "American Indians" are usually non-earthlings (though generally pretty humanoid in appearance) who assist the "Indians" in some manner or receive survival, spiritual, or supernatural help from the "Indians."

Or the "Indian" as the "alien other" in science fiction serves a similar purpose to real, live "Indians" on display in the nineteenth century at world fairs such as the World's Columbian Exposition of 1893 or expositions such as the Philadelphia Centennial Exposition and the International Exhibition, both held in 1876. These exhibits were designed to present American inventions and technological progress as "the universal 'law of life,'" in which "primitive" First Nations "technologies such as weapons and tools highlighted the (white) nation's achievements by showing how far civilization had evolved in relation to 'less developed' (usually a synonym for nonwhite) peoples, civilization's still living ancestors."[1] No distinction was made between the different First Nations artifacts. All were attributed to a "collective Indian," and as Robert Rydell has observed:

The central conception underlying the Indian exhibit at the Centennial, in short, was that Native American cultures and people belonged to the interminable wasteland of humanity's dark and stormy beginnings. The Indians' worth as human beings was determined by their usefulness as counterpoint to the unfolding progress of the ages.[2]

With a few strategic alterations of phrases in Rydell's statement, the "Indian" as "alien other" appears:

The central conception underlying the Indian in outer space or encountered on an alien planet is that Native American cultures and people belong to the interminable wasteland of an alien race's dark and stormy beginnings. The Indians' worth as alien beings is determined by their usefulness as counterpoint to humanity's unfolding progress of the ages.

Tasiwoopa ápi explains:

As of 2003, we [First Nations peoples] are still considered and openly viewed by the dominant society as the "Indian alien other" because we try to cling to as many of our ancient ways as we can because it is who we are. It gives us identity. But in doing so, we refuse to slip into the "melting pot"—to use their terms. Just like the dominant society wanted to put their thumbprint on our ways, in order that we could be more acceptable to them, we have acquiesced to the dominant society by putting our music and our words to their songs such as hymns and Christmas music sung in our native languages. We attach our ideology and our ceremonial thumbprint to the dominant society's religions in order that the dominant society will assume that we have accepted their ways and they will leave us alone. We have learned their language so that we can communicate with their legal system and, more importantly, so we can communicate with their academics, who appear to be our worst enemy. As an example, we have learned to study the pedagogical ontogogy of hegemony in order to begin the process of understanding how the white man really works. Because education has not changed with regard to Indigenous peoples, in particular those living on what is now known as the North American continent, we continue to be viewed as "alien others" while we have been forced, as a people, on a macro scale not only to understand how the dominant society functions but to learn to work within, beside, and around the dominant society in order simply to survive—never mind to grow, to increase our population, and to rebuild our societies to what they were. Our cultures have and will remain alien to the dominant society; therefore we, too, have always been and always will be aliens who do not conform to white social norms in our religious beliefs and our daily lives. Thus we fit perfectly into the role of aliens just about anywhere, including science fiction.[3]

The first portion of this chapter contains a synopsis and textual analysis of three science fiction TV shows that aired between 1965 and 1995, illustrating "Indians" in primarily nonspiritual, day-to-day living situations. The episodes are arranged chronologically: *My Favorite Martian* "Go West, Young Martian, Go West, Part II," which aired in 1965; *Star Trek* "The Paradise Syndrome," which aired in 1968; and *Star Trek: Voyager* "Tattoo," which aired in 1995. The second portion of the chapter presents both the amusement and the trepidation expressed by First Nations peoples after watching "all-purpose Hollywood Indians" in futuristic and time travel settings.[4] The chapter ends with hypotheses based on the expressed observations of the participants.

My Favorite Martian "Go West, Young Martian, Go West, Part II"

In "Part I" of the *My Favorite Martian* episode called "Go West, Young Martian, Go West" (1965),[5] Detective Bill Brennan finds and accidentally activates a time machine belonging to Uncle Martin.[6] He and Tim travel back in time to St. Louis in 1849. Although the time machine moves through time, it remains in place, in the field where Tim's apartment in Los Angeles will later be built. While pondering how to reach the time machine, the pair buy lunch. Unfortunately, they pay for it with modern money and get tossed into jail by Brennan's great-grandfather, Marshal Will Brennan, for passing counterfeit money. Uncle Martin uses the time to draw a map of the location of the time machine in case he and Tim get separated. Then Uncle Martin uses his Martian powers in his index finger to break them out of jail. Escaping on a riverboat, they meet Lorelei Glutz, the great-grandmother of Mrs. Brown and rescue her from thieves. Uncle Martin and Tim, however, get blamed for the theft and are recaptured by Marshal Brennan.

As the story continues in "Part II," Uncle Martin and Tim escape jail again, only to be assaulted by the thieves, who steal the map because they believe it will lead to a gold mine. Lorelei, who has joined a wagon train headed for the rich California gold fields, finds Uncle Martin and Tim and gets them on the wagon train as her guides. The thieves capture her en route. Uncle Martin uses his Martian powers of telepathy to discover the whereabouts of Lorelei. The thieves are about to break camp when the pair arrive. Tim points out that the thieves have the advantage, as they have weapons and Tim and Uncle Martin don't. But Uncle Martin is unconcerned:

UNCLE MARTIN: We have far greater weapons to turn against them—their own minds. . . . A well-aimed shot of disillusionary illusion should send them running. Fear, Tim, is a much more destructive force than gunpowder.

Uncle Martin digs in his mental "historical motion picture bank" and projects a dinosaur to scares the thieves away. Then Uncle Martin and Tim free Lorelei. The thieves run off so fast they leave their horses, their tack, and the map in one of the saddlebags. But just as Tim finds it, warriors in face paint appear on the rim of nearby cliffs. At first, Tim thinks they are more of Uncle Martin's motion picture bank and asks him to turn it off. Uncle Martin assures Tim that he is not projecting anything. Tim points to the cliffs and tells Uncle Martin to gaze at the reality along the ridgeline.

Five half-dressed warriors, each sporting a headband with a single feather sticking up, draw their bows and arrows. The three whites end up as prisoners in the "Indian" camp with teepees and an all-male group of Natives sitting on logs around a fire. It is daytime. A "medicine man," complete with a horned buffalo headdress, dances around the fire, singing and shaking a rattle shaped like a miniature horned buffalo head. The "chief" perches on a log in full regalia, which includes a full-length war bonnet and a feathered lance. The "Indians" whoop, and a drum beats in the background at an incredibly fast pace for the "medicine man" dancer to keep up with.

One "Indian" stands guard outside the teepee where Uncle Martin and Tim are being held, with their hands tied behind them. Tim doesn't like the song. Uncle Martin, who understands the language, although not as well as he understands Comanche, tells Tim that the song is a death song—theirs.

Getting frustrated, Tim demands that Uncle Martin explain that they are friendly:

UNCLE MARTIN: . . . these are Yuma Indians, one of the most treacherous tribes in the West. They aren't interested in developing their social life.

Uncle Martin figures that if they are to have any chance at all, he must get away and somehow persuade the "medicine man" to release them. So Uncle Martin again uses his Martian powers through his index finger, this time to levitate the knife from the "Indian" guard's belt. The guard pays no attention to the knife and only scratches a spot where the knife slides past his rib cage as it goes to Uncle Martin. Wiggling his index finger, Uncle Martin gets the knife to cut the ropes binding him. He leaves Tim tied up and raises his antennae, becoming invisible. The Yumas don't even notice that Uncle Martin is missing when they shove the captured Marshal Brennan inside the teepee with Tim. The marshal, who has been chasing the pair of time travelers since they arrived in St. Louis, assumes that Uncle Martin got away from the "savages" and saved his own hide. The marshal thinks that Uncle Martin and Tim are outlaws and cowards.

Outside the teepee, the warriors whoop louder and the medicine man's dance becomes frenzied. Amid his song and dance, he gets on his knees, looks up at the noonday sky, raises both hands skyward, and prays to "Wana Tanka." That's when Uncle Martin reappears, dressed in buckskins, Apache boots, a beaded necklace, long black braids, and a mask that looks like a mixture of African and modern art—with black horns, a red sun spot on the forehead, and "Indian" face paint in stripes on the cheeks and the bridge of the nose. In "Indian grunt-speak" Uncle Martin motions for all the Yuma men to gather before him. The "medicine man" shakes his rattle at Uncle Martin as if to ward off evil, but he complies.

The warrior guarding the prisoners enters the teepee and announces in broken English that the "Great Warrior Spirit" has come for the "palefaces." He expresses no emotion when he discovers that Uncle Martin has escaped.

All the prisoners, including Lorelei, are hustled before the "chief," the "medicine man," and Uncle Martin, who is dressed up as the supernatural warrior Sun God. The guard explains that the "other paleface" escaped. This sends all the "Indians" to their feet, whooping. At this point Uncle Martin switches to speaking to the Yumas in English. He also mutters his true identity to Tim, who questions why the Martian is decked out in "Indian" clothes and a strange mask, and the following conversation takes place:

UNCLE MARTIN: Playing the Great Warrior Spirit come down in person to get his sacrifices.

MEDICINE MAN: (Lifting Lorelei's hair as the Warrior Spirit approaches) Golden hair hangs nice from Warrior Spirit belt.

LORELEI: . . . I bet you tell that to all the squaws.

UNCLE MARTIN: I'll take all three of them.

MEDICINE MAN: But what of other paleface who ran away? You wait. We catch.

UNCLE MARTIN: Forget him. You can owe me one. (Raising his hand) How!

With classic Hollywood "Indian" music, Uncle Martin leads Lorelei, Tim, and Brennan away from camp. But the marshal decides that the spirit isn't going to succeed at marching him "out to get scalped," and he tackles the spirit. The mask and wig come off, revealing Uncle Martin to the Yumas, who are sitting on a log, chatting and laughing with the "medicine man." As the Yumas realize they have been duped and race toward the prisoners, Uncle Martin directs Brennan to take Lorelei and a couple of horses belonging to the Yumas and to head for Fort Yuma. He and Tim will hold off the "Indians."

Uncle Martin points his index finger at the approaching Yumas, freezing them. When Tim asks how long that will hold them, Uncle Martin replies that the freezing won't last long in the heat. They take two more horses that have "Indian" blankets thrown over Western saddles and ride off.

They pass a herd of brown and white cattle and a covered wagon. "Indian" scouts on the hillside motion to a group of warriors, using their rifles that have a feather sticking out of the gun barrel, and the chase is on. Bare-chested braves, whooping and carrying feather-decorated rifles and lances, pursue the two time travelers, who easily give the "Indians" the slip.

Meanwhile, Lorelei and Brennan arrive safely at the fort. The colonel assures the marshal that Lorelei will reach her destination safely. Brennan then requests that the colonel give him a detail of men so he can round up his prisoners (Uncle Martin and Tim), provided "the Injins" don't reach them before the cavalry does. Lorelei protests, since Uncle Martin and Tim helped them escape from the "Indians." Condescendingly, the marshal puts his arm around her and touches her chin, telling her that a man of the law has a dirty job to do, but an important one.

So, with quasi-Superman music, the "Indians" race toward Uncle Martin and Tim from one direction, and the U.S. Cavalry advances from the opposite direction. The two time travelers hurriedly search for the time machine in an open field where their apartment will be in the future. Uncle Martin senses the approach of the "Indians" and the cavalry, and he freezes both for a few minutes while they find the time machine, which he calls the CCTBS. Uncle Martin hopes that the elements in the machine have not been corroded. The "Indians" and the cavalry unfreeze and charge forward. Uncle Martin throws the switch on the machine. In a puff of smoke, he and Tim land back at their Los Angeles apartment.

Overexposure has worn the CCTBS, causing short circuits, but it can be repaired. Tim decides to take a hot shower, and Uncle Martin takes a couple of steaks out of the freezer to barbecue. Tim calls from the bedroom, asking Uncle Martin how long it will take to fix the time machine. Uncle Martin says a couple of weeks. Tim suggests that he set a third place at the table, for there is a worn-out "Indian" on a spotted horse in the living room that had been caught in their return to the present.

The setting for *My Favorite Martian* and Mrs. Brown's home and garage apartment where Tim and Uncle Martian lived was Los Angeles, California, Hollywood's mainstay location of the time. Every writer who ever attended a writers' conference or picked up a book about writing has been bombarded with the advice "write what you know." Therefore a Hollywood writer writing about a favorite Hollywood setting would, most likely, be writing a script incorporating familiar elements of local history. Associate producer and script consultant Marty Roth may not have been very knowledgeable about Southern California's "Indian" history, and as Mihesuah has pointed out, there is a "legacy of misinformation . . . about the non-European segments of our society" taught in schools across America.[7] But in the 1960s, when this episode of *My Favorite Martian* was produced, Euro-American history of the gold rush invasion of California would have been easily accessible through a local call to the nearest library or university history department. This episode, unfortunately, showcased the fact that Hollywood writers, directors, and producers did not have a grasp even of white history, let alone of "Indian" history. For example, Fort Yuma was located in the extreme southeastern edge of California in the 1960s, but the fort was not called a fort, let alone named Fort Yuma in 1849.[8]

On 2 October 1849 the U.S. military established Camp Calhoun on the Spanish Mission site of Puerto de la Purísima Concepción, a mesa on the Rio Colorado that is currently the border between California and Arizona. Both states claim the fort, for Major Samuel P. Heintzelman relocated the camp late in 1850, calling it Camp Independence.[9] The following spring, the camp moved back to the previous position and was renamed Camp Yuma, after the Native nation living nearby.[10] Unfortunately, herein lies what Strickland refers to as Hollywood's "most bizarre sense of geography and culture, particularly of Indian cultures."[11] The location of what would become Fort Yuma in the 1850s is nearly 200 miles away from Los Angeles as the crow flies. Moreover, the Yumas would have been chasing Uncle Martin and Tim from the same direction as the Fourth Infantry—from the east. The Yumas and the soldiers would not have come from opposing directions, with Uncle Martin and Tim caught in the middle in the vicinity of their LA apartment, because during the 1849 time frame of "Go West, Young Martian, Go West" the Yumas inhabited "the valleys of the lower Colorado and Gila rivers," primarily in current Arizona.[12] When this episode aired, the Yumas—who prefer to be called by their correct name, Quechan—were living on the Cocopah Indian Reservation in the southwestern portion of Arizona, as well as the Fort Yuma–Quechan Reservation.[13]

Additionally, the cliché of the "Indians" versus the U.S. Cavalry cannot be ignored. But those responsible for this version of the classic stereotype actually—and, in all probability, accidentally, considering their general lack of knowledge concerning U.S. military history—placed the correct army unit at Fort Yuma. First Nations and military historian Tasiwoopa ápi explains:

> In watching the old series reruns, it is a true quirk of circumstance that the wardrobe designers chose to use the post–Civil War Fourth Infantry insignia on the uniforms of the Cavalry. It is ironic that this unit, who appear to be dedicated to the eradication of the Indian, would in World War II specifically enlist Indians to use their language to help win the war, in particular the Comanches, who were critical to the war in the European theater from D-Day to VE-Day.[14]

Again following the hackneyed image of the "savage Indian of the movie Western,"[15] Uncle Martin in the *My Favorite Martian* episode pronounced the Yumas, like the Comanches, to be "one of the most treacherous tribes in the West." According to Gibson, however, the Yumas were "peaceful agricultural Indians" who raised crops such as corn, squash, beans, sunflower seeds, and cotton in the desert environment and had "only limited defensive weapons" to use against the "Intruder Peoples" such as the Apaches.[16]

Being desert dwellers, the Yuma people would have died out from heatstroke long before the Euro-Americans arrived, had they actually dressed in the typical homogenized Hollywood "Plains Indian" garb featured in the *My Favorite Martian* episode. Instead, Yumas wore little clothing in the hot weather—the men wore a skin breechclout, and the women wore a bark or plant fiber "dress" or "double apron"—and all went barefoot or wore sandals made out of rawhide or bark.[17]

Nor did Yumas wear feathered war bonnets, as depicted in the episode. In fact, when Twentieth Century Fox hired Arizona First Nations individuals to portray "Plains Indians" in the 1944 film *Buffalo Bill*, wardrobe staff had to instruct the Indigenous actors in "how to wear the feathered headdress, leather breeches, and fringed leather shirts"— they "didn't think this was the kind of thing to wear in that summer heat, but they put their costumes on uncomplainingly."[18]

Hollywood writers, directors, and producers, however, missed a chance to further another "Indian" stereotype in the *My Favorite Martian* episode—that of the "unwashed, unclean heathen."[19] Huntington reported that the Yumas were "very filthy in their habits," for they coated their heads and bodies with mud to protect their skin from bit-ing insects.[20] This strategy wasn't technologically advanced by Martian or even Euro-American standards, but it worked.

On the other hand, Uncle Martin, the Martian alien other, possessed a "vast storehouse of advanced technological knowledge."[21] These allowed him to place a unique twist on some very old Hollywood "Indian" stereotypes. For instance, Uncle Martin continued the long Hollywood tradition of freezing "Indians" in time, except that he did it literally with his magic-powered finger.

The Martian easily duped the "ignorant savages," who practiced a primitive, superstitious religion based on human sacrifice. The Time-Life book *The Indians* classified acts of "human sacrifice" as "major ceremonies" for Plains Indians that were, to "Indians," "natural and necessary in order to avert disaster and maintain their well-being" and "were supposed to redound to the good of the whole village."[22] Such stereotypical images of the Indigenous population, as previously discussed, have been passed down from generation to generation of Euro-American children and accepted as fact, however erroneous, not only appearing in colonial newspapers and magazines but also in American history textbooks for centuries.[23]

Another area where the Martian's technology gave him the advantage was his ability to disappear and then reappear in front of the "medicine man," scaring the Natives into believing him to be a god—a forerunner to the *Star Trek* episode "The Paradise Syndrome"—and in the Martian's ability to levitate objects and thus free himself. This was the classic stereotype of "the Indian offering hope of an earlier natural age to the white man enslaved by technology."[24]

Depicting First Nations individuals as gullible and ignorant and therefore easy to manipulate also dates back to early federal government relationships with the First Nations. The European and American governments insisted on maintaining a wardship over Natives, whom whites perceived as "children of the forest" who needed a parental figure to manage their affairs and land.[25] The stereotype of the simpleminded, easily duped "Indian" arose from the practice of wardship.[26]

Star Trek "The Paradise Syndrome"

In the *Star Trek* episode "The Paradise Syndrome" (1968), Captain Kirk, Mr. Spock, and Dr. McCoy beam down to a planet with earthlike vegetation that is about to be destroyed by an asteroid. The three Star Fleet officers come across an obelisk, made from an unknown metal, that is covered with unidentified writing—which is not all that unusual for this space-traveling crew. But when they go to "find out what life-forms are blessed by this environment," as Kirk says, the crew encounter people far more alien to the planet than the obelisk:

MCCOY: Why they look like—I'd swear they're American Indians.
SPOCK: They are, doctor. A mixture of Navajo, Mohegan, and Delaware, I believe. All among the more advanced and peaceful tribes.

Maintaining their distance, the three observe the "Indians," dressed in buckskins and going about their daily lives in the village, which is an amalgamation of teepees and a Haudenosaunee longhouse set right on the edge of a lake of pristine blue water. Kirk comments that the setting appears similar to the mythical locations of Atlantis or Shangri-la. He wishes they could stay awhile in the peaceful surrounds instead of having to warp out of orbit in an attempt to divert the asteroid that is on a collision course with the planet.

While Spock and McCoy take a few final tricorder readings, Kirk goes back to the obelisk for one last look. When he opens his communicator and signals the ship, a trapdoor in the obelisk slides opens and Kirk falls in. As he stands up, he inadvertently activates a memory sequence device that is part of the machine inside. It knocks him unconscious. Crew members conduct an unsuccessful search for their captain, but time is against them. Reluctantly, they must leave orbit in order to divert the asteroid.

Kirk regains consciousness, but he can't remember anything. When he emerges from the obelisk, two young Native women are in the process of laying baskets of food and flowers at the base of the structure. He wants to know who the women are, and one answers, "We are your people. We've been waiting for you to come to us."

Kirk goes before the unnamed chief and the "medicine chief" Salish, who demands that Kirk prove himself to be the god the chief says was promised by "the wise ones who planted us here"—the one who would come to save the people and would rouse the "temple's spirit and make the sky grow quiet." Of course, Kirk is unsure who he himself is, but he does recall that he came from the sky as well as from the obelisk. Then the "priestess" Miramanee and a man bring in a boy who was caught up in fishnets and drowned. After Salish pronounces the boy dead, Kirk administers CPR, reviving the boy. The chief declares, "Only a god can breath life into the dead" and tells Salish to give his "medicine badge" to Kirk.

Later, when Miramanee is attending to the "god's" needs, Kirk asks her to tell him about the "Wise Ones" who brought the people to the planet.

MIRAMANEE: The Wise Ones brought us here from far away. They chose a medicine chief to keep the secret of the temple and to use it when the sky darkens.

KIRK: . . . The secrets are passed on from father to son. Why doesn't Salish use it? Why are the people in danger?

MIRAMANEE: His father did not wish to share his power too soon. He died before he told Salish the secret.

Meanwhile, the chief voices his concern that they have displeased the god Kirok, as Kirk is now known, that they have "not improved as quickly as the Wise Ones wish." Kirk responds, "Your land is rich, your people happy. Who could be displeased with that?"

Kirk admits that he is happy and peaceful for the first time in his life, but that's just the beginning of his pleasure. Shortly thereafter, he learns that tribal tradition and tribal law give Kirk the chief's daughter and "priestess" Miramanee in marriage. Salish, however, intercepts Kirk on the way to the "joining" ceremony. The two fight, and Salish makes Kirk bleed. Salish vows to prove to his people that Kirk is no god. The joining, however, takes place.

Meanwhile, the crew of the *Enterprise* fail to deflect the asteroid and limp back to the planet just four hours ahead of it. This takes two months. During that time, Kirk settles into married life by showing the "Indians" how to double their food supply by building irrigation ditches from the lake to the fields, how to extend the day by using lamps, and how to use cooking and preserving techniques so that the extra food being grown will sustain the people in "times of famine."

When signs of the impending asteroid collision start—wind, thunder, darkening sky, trembling ground—the people expect the god Kirok to save them. When Kirk cannot get back into the obelisk to make the "blue flame" that will save their world, the people stone him and Miramanee, who is pregnant with Kirk's child.

McCoy and Spock beam down, frightening the "Indian" mob away from the obelisk. Spock has deciphered some of the symbols on the obelisk, enough to know that it is an asteroid deflector and that access can be gained by playing a series of musical notes, or "tonal qualities." He asks Miramanee why the people were stoning them, and she responds that they were angry because Kirok couldn't get back into the "temple."

Kirk still can't remember how he got into the obelisk, so Spock performs a Vulcan "mind meld" to give Kirk his memory back. Once the two get inside, Spock reads the notes and pushes the button to send the blue beam shooting out of the obelisk to push the asteroid away from the planet.

In true "Hollywood Indian" tradition, Miramanee dies because she has broken the old Hollywood morality code of "no miscegenation" by marrying a white man.[27] Such a marriage, however, is acceptable because she is a priestess, the daughter of the chief (the "Indian princess"), and also because she dies.[28] Kirk suffers no consequences, other than one brief moment of sadness before he and his crew leave paradise and its "primitive" inhabitants behind, because of yet another "Hollywood Indian" tradition. As Friar and Friar put it, "white men have lusted after Indian maids since the [movie camera] cranks started turning," but "there was to be no happy hanky-panky between the races."[29]

This episode also perpetuates the classic Hollywood "children of the forest" stereotype, in which "Indians" never progress beyond their "primitive" or "natural" state.[30] Through Hollywood's eyes, "Indians" are seen as "forever stuck in the nineteenth century."[31] As Francis Parkman once stated, the Native "will not learn the arts of civilization, and he and his forest must perish together"[32]—unless the "Indians" are rescued by the "Wise Ones" and safely tucked away on some distant reservation away from the white man's interference, as in "The Paradise Syndrome."

Spock claims that one of the groups in this unlikely mixture of "Indians" found on this planet belongs to the Navajo Nation, the dominant society's name for the Diné. The "Indians," however, are depicted in this episode as possessing no livestock, for no evidence of sheep raising or wool blanket making is shown. Thus, the Diné portion of this group would have had to have been plucked from their ancestral homelands sometime prior to the early 1600s, when the Diné were still a hunter-gatherer culture and had not yet been exposed to the Spanish invaders, who forced Christianity and a pastoral lifestyle on the First Nations peoples of what is now the American Southwest.[33]

The original *Star Trek* series was set in the twenty-third century, raising the question of how a culture could remain stagnant from the 1600s to the 2200s. The very act of bringing together people from three distinct nations, to say nothing of transporting them to another planet on a spaceship (which is discussed below), would have to have some discernible impact on their descendants' culture—other than shortening the hemlines on the buckskin dresses and adding elasticized beaded headbands straight out of Hollywood's costume designers' idea of "Indian" clothing, which bears little resemblance to the type of clothing worn by the Delawares, the Diné, or the Mohegans.[34] When the Diné and the Apaches settled near the Pueblo peoples, some intertribal marriages took place, as did some absorption of aspects of the Pueblo culture and worldviews,[35] but no such exchange appears in the mixing of the Delawares, Diné, and Mohegans in this *Star Trek* episode.

This brings up another stereotype in the episode, that of the "homogenized Indian."[36] "The Paradise Syndrome" lumps diverse cultures and peoples living in diverse climates into one "all-purpose Hollywood Indian."[37] Alanson Skinner offered an accurate assessment of these stereotypical portrayals in 1914. He called them "ethnographically grotesque farces" in which "Delawares are dressed as Sioux and the Indians of Manhattan Island are shown dwelling in skin teepees of the type used only by the tribes beyond the Mississippi."[38] Hollywood had always chosen to overlook such "ethnographically grotesque farces," and the writers, directors, and producers of the original *Star Trek* series were simply carrying on the old Hollywood tradition.

Nevertheless, Hollywood was evidently up on current events in one area. Seven years prior to the airing of this episode, a preliminary report issued by the Commission on the Rights, Liberties, and Responsibilities of the American Indian used a quote that states, "Indians believe they have values worth preserving," and the commission, in a radical change of direction from the U.S. Indian policies of the day, agreed with those First Nations peoples.[39] "The Paradise Syndrome" manifested this idea via the "Preservers."

Star Trek: Voyager "Tattoo"

As the first officer aboard the Federation starship *Voyager*, the character Chakotay, played by non–First Nations actor Robert Beltran, is the first "Native American" crew member shown in the *Star Trek* universe. Chakotay also represents the only First Nations character ever portrayed on a weekly American science fiction television series. The "Tattoo" episode aired in 1995 during *Star Trek: Voyager*'s second season.[40]

In this episode, Chakotay leads an away mission on a moon in the Delta Quadrant and finds a chahmoozee, a very old symbol of healing, which he believes was etched into the moon's surface to serve as atonement for injuring the land with a campfire. He bases this idea on flashbacks to his boyhood days when his father, Kolopak, took young Chakotay to the Central American rain forest in search of the descendants of their own ancestors—the Rubber Tree People.[41] Kolopak tells his son that the descendants of the ancient Rubber Tree People have never left the jungle, rarely intermarry with other Indigenous people, and have chosen to follow the old ways, such as using firewood instead of twenty-fourth-century fuels and traveling on foot rather than using transports. Kolopak tells the teenager they follow these traditions out of respect to "the Sky Spirits," the ones who guided their ancestors to the land that would become the tribe's sacred place. Chakotay is skeptical.

Back in the present, Chakotay explains to his captain that his father made him leave their home colony, which was close to the Cardassian border, leaving behind his friends and his home in order to go on a silly quest for their ancestors deep in the wretched jungles of Central America. It seems that Chakotay's father had spent many years searching for the descendants of their people, the Rubber Tree People, and his father was disappointed that Chakotay did not share this passion for their ancestors.

Chakotay and Captain Janeway compare a picture of the chahmoozee carved into a river stone that Chakotay keeps in his medicine bundle with the one he found on the moon surface nearly 70,000 miles away in the Delta Quadrant. She asks him to speculate on how this same symbol could be found on opposite sides of the galaxy.

CHAKOTAY: I can give you an official Rubber Tree People theory—Sky Spirits . . . It's an ancient myth. Sky Spirits from Above created the first Rubber People in their own image and led the way to a sacred land where the Rubber People could live for eternity.

The people who left the chahmoozee symbol also left a "warp signature" that trailed away from the moon surface, and because the *Voyager* crew now need minerals to seal their own warp coils, they decide to follow the trail in hopes that the aliens' technology can help the *Voyager* crew.

When the crew reach the aliens' planet, they can't beam down, because each time they select a site, a storm forms above it. The shuttle also experiences storms as the Away Team enters the planet's atmosphere. Chakotay flashes back to another storm in the rain forest, where he complained to his father about the inhospitable location where it rained all the time and there were lots of bugs in a very hot climate.

In the flashback, Kolopak tries to explain that the Sky Spirits revere the land and all life-forms and that the people should make friends with the natural world, which also includes the bugs. Chakotay wants none of that, which leads him to express sorrow over not being the kind of son his father wants. With patience and typical stoicism, Kolopak explains that he always knew his son would be difficult, as he had been a breech birth, which meant that "the spirits had chosen you to be a Contrary."

Chakotay insists that he makes his own decisions and he doesn't care if that means he is a Contrary. He is none too pleased when his father concludes that the boy will become lost with no guiding spirit to advise him.

The Away Team lands in a jungle terrain similar to that of Chakotay's ancestors. A hawk flies overhead, and Chakotay remembers his father's asking what the hawks say to the teen. Chakotay hears nothing and tells his father of his plans to go to Star Fleet Academy.

KOLOPAK: Well, you've never fully embraced the traditions of our tribe. I know that. You've always been curious about other societies, and that is why I allowed you to read about it because I believe ignorance is our greatest enemy. But to leave the tribe!

CHAKOTAY: Our tribe lives in the past. A past of fantasy and myth.

Kolopak reminds his son that there is no escaping their past or their heritage, no matter how hard they may try. At this point, Chakotay points out that other Native peoples have accepted and adapted to living in the twenty-fourth century. His father informs him that a fifteen-year-old youth has no place questioning the decision of the tribe's elders.

KOLOPAK: You will never belong to that other life. And if you leave, you will never belong to this one. You'll be caught between worlds.

A hawk attacks *Voyager* crew member Neelix when he discovers a structure similar to the one Chakotay and his father found in the jungle back on Earth.[42] Although the structure shows signs of recent occupation, the Away Team members can't find the people by using their tricorders. Chakotay tells the others to lay down their weapons. Crew member Tuvok objects but complies.[43] In another flashback, Chakotay remembers that once his father and the others had laid down their weapons, saying that the Rubber Tree People had reason to be afraid, as their history, like other Indigenous peoples' history, is satiated with conquest and subjugators who had enslaved entire Indigenous populations and brought death and terrible disease in their wake. Speaking the ancient language, Kolopak says they came in peace, and the Rubber Tree People had come out of the jungle, curious as to why Kolopak knew their ancient chahmoozee symbol, which he drew in the dirt, and their language.

Back in the present, a windstorm comes up suddenly, and the Away Team heads back to the shuttle. A tree falls on Chakotay and knocks him out. The others call the ship for an emergency beam out, leaving Chakotay behind. When Chakotay regains consciousness, he returns to the structure and disrobes, saying, as well as showing, that the people have nothing to fear from him. He finds a garment and puts it on. His father had donned the clothes of their cousins, the Rubber Tree People, and even got their customary face tattoo. The young Chakotay had wanted nothing to do with the whole thing.

Meanwhile, Tuvok explains to the captain that someone on the planet is manipulating the weather in order to keep them off the surface. Captain Janeway decides to land the ship on the surface in order to retrieve Chakotay, facing a storm that threatens to wreck the ship.

On the surface, Chakotay faces his own storm at the entrance of a cave, where he encounters the people who speak the ancient language. Chakotay apologizes for not knowing the language and not understanding them. All he can say is "chahmoozee." After seeing the face tattoo, the alien gives Chakotay a device that allows him to communicate with the alien, who wants to know about the tattoo. Chakotay explains that he wears it in honor of his father, who in turn wore one in honor of their ancestors.

ALIEN: We were taught all of them had been annihilated. We were taught your world had been ravaged by those with no respect for life or land. . . . (He turns to the other aliens.) He claims to be a descendant of the Inheritors.

The alien explains that his people originally visited Earth 45,000 years ago and encountered nomadic hunters who had "no spoken language, no culture except the use of fire and stone weapons, but they did have a respect for the land and other living creatures that impressed us deeply." The aliens gave these hunters "an inheritance, a genetic bonding so that they might thrive and protect your world." On later visits, the aliens learned that their gift inspired the hunters to migrate away from their frozen land to an "unpeopled land," taking a thousand generations to cross the new "unpeopled land." Then new people invaded and brought death and disease. On their last visit, twelve generations ago, the aliens could find no indication of the Inheritors' existence left on Earth. The aliens, whom Chakotay's people called the Sky Spirits, had hidden when *Voyager* arrived, believing the humans had come to wipe out their people too.

Chakotay explains that *Voyager* is on a mission of peace and exploration, but the alien insists that many conquerors have come before who claimed to be on journeys of nothing more than peaceful exploration. Chakotay assures the alien that Earthlings have changed since the last time their two peoples encountered each other.

The storm dissipates around the ship, and the crew locate Chakotay. The aliens let the crew have some of the minerals they need. Chakotay wishes he could see his father's face, explaining that Kolopak died fighting the Cardassians and that the he and his father were not on good terms at the time. Chakotay continued the fight in honor of his father and "spoke to him in my vision quests, but he never answered until now." Now Chakotay hears what the hawk says—that Chakotay is home.

According to the official *Star Trek: Voyager* episode guide,[44] Chakotay's™ people and their cousins, the Rubber Tree People, are supposedly descendant of "(pre)Mayans." Yet Chakotay's culture, as portrayed in the series, provides a perfect example of the generic "Indian" culture found in early American newspapers, where many individual cultures were merged into a single "Indian" culture. The first season saw Chakotay practicing a very Hollywood version of Plains-culture religion, when he used a "medicine bundle" and a high-tech device that acted like instant peyote to summon his "spirit guide"[45] (see chapter 5 for a more detailed discussion of Chakotay's "medicine bundle" in the episode "The Cloud"). Additionally, Chakotay possessed a "personal medicine wheel" that resembled a stylized compass and supposedly promoted self-healing.[46] In an episode titled "Cathexis," Chakotay uses his "Indian" powers of the "medicine wheel" to help the crew, thus becoming the "good Indian" in the classic Pocahontas sense. All these "Indian" trappings are as much a Euro-American fantasy of First Nations cultures as the 1760 account of the Mohawk cannibal mentioned in chapter 2.

Furthermore, considering that Chakotay is the only First Nations role model around in a futuristic setting, it's unfortunate that the Hollywood producers decided that the role should be played by a non–First Nations actor. Not only does Robert Beltran dismiss Chakotay's position as a role model for young First Nations peoples, but falling back on the standard "skulking" "Noble Redman" stereotypes in a live chat online in 1999, Beltran characterized Chakotay as "limp, weasely, cowardly, homosexual, charming."[47]

First Nations Peoples' Assessment of Futuristic "Indian" Stereotypes

In the *My Favorite Martian* episode discussed above, the customary Hollywood "warpath" consisted of the classic clash of "Indians" with the U.S. Cavalry in the Old West, with a time traveler and a Martian thrown in for science fiction flavor. First Nations viewers generally disliked this portrayal of Natives, cutting it little slack for being written and produced nearly forty years ago. "Despite the film being made in the 1960s," wrote one woman, "it is full of discrepancies. I could sit here all day and point them out."[48] Another stated, "I dislike this film clip because it shows Indians frozen in time. People tend to think that Natives have not advanced technologically in the last 1000 years. I feel this shows a real negative image toward Native Americans."[49]

Another individual connected the Hollywood stereotype of technologically advanced whites versus the low to no technology of First

Nations, as demonstrated in this episode, with the origins of this stereotype:

The philosophes of the Enlightenment promoted modern technology, but, at the same time, they moaned about the loss of mankind's innocence and man's almost childlike way of viewing the world—the "natural state" of man, I believe they called it. That was why they were so fascinated with and fixated on us. The Natives of North America represented a "paradise lost" to the so-called modern, technologically advanced Europeans. Why else do Europeans and Euro-Americans persist in dressing up and "playing Indian" to this day? However, at the same time, this same people just love to feel so superior to Natives because they continue to see us as children of nature who have no real place in the modern world—except to entertain them with our quaint customs and "costumes." And Hollywood gives whites a constant diet of childish, easily tricked Indians.[50]

Or as one man pointed out:

There were two images: the idea that the medicine man could be duped by technology and the last scene of the whipped Indian on the horse. Those are the two that stand out. The fact that once again here's the dumb Indian getting tricked by the white man, an alien, where he is, in fact, the one in the flesh hauling off the prisoners.[51]

One participant summarized:

Here is the image of the uncivilized savages and the white captives being held at their camp. The Martian uses his power to impersonate a powerful spirit god against the Indians' primitive spiritual beliefs; and tricks them into allowing the captives to be released. Not much in the way of positive images of the Indian culture here.[52]

This impression of the "Indians" appearing as simpletons garnered additional negative commentary. One man likened it to "a mockery" in which the "Indian also seem to be always gullible, which in turn makes Indians look dumb."[53] Another found it frustrating that "people still perceived us as barbaric and just wanting to be mean to the white man."[54] "I didn't like this clip because it demonstrated how easily tricked Indians supposedly are because of their beliefs," stated one woman.[55]

Another participant discussed not only the not-so-noble "Indian" stereotype but also the persistence of Hollywood to stick all Natives into a single "Indian" culture.

Move over Tonto! This episode is Hollywood fakery at its worst. Even though it is very much a product of its time, I find it offensive—mainly because Hollywood persists today in using many of the tired, old stereotypes seen in this 1960s episode. How many centuries will have to pass before non-Natives start to realize that we have and always have had complex cultures? Why are Natives forever shown as revenge seekers, out to rape, pillage, and massacre innocents—especially blonde white women? When whites and Natives clash, whites always have some trick up their sleeve to get them out of a jam or the Cavalry always comes to the rescue. Indians don't go around capturing whites all the time, but that's exactly the impression people get from watching TV shows that have Indians in them.[56]

Hollywood, following in the steps of newspapers, magazines, and books, has routinely ignored the diversity of hundreds of distinctly different Native cultures, as well as numerous other historical facts. For example, many white women captured by "Indians" preferred the freedoms and privileges they experienced living among First Nations peoples, such as having a voice in how things would be done that was actually listened to by the men. Women in matrilineal and matrilocal tribes such as the Haudenosaunee nations of the northeast and the Cherokees of the southeast controlled the land and the food supply, children belonged to the mother's clan, and women had a voice in the government.[57] "I think that they're [Hollywood is] making Indians seem like they go and capture white people to kill them or hold them hostage or to do harm," criticized one participant.[58] Added another, "If the blonde woman [Lorelei] had a brain in her head, which she obviously didn't, she might have discovered she liked the liberated lifestyle of Native women and decided to not continue West with that arrogant jerk, the marshal. I don't suppose Hollywood writers have ever heard of Mary Jemison!"[59]

Mary Jemison, who was taken captive in 1758 by the Shawnees, explained that she was formally adopted by a Seneca family in place of a son lost during the French and Indian War.[60] Although she had several opportunities to return to white society, she chose to remain with the Senecas, becoming a wife and a mother in an atmosphere where "wants were few, and easily satisfied," life was "a continual round of pleasures," and wives "attended to agriculture, their families, and a few domestic concerns of small consequence, and attended with but little labor."[61] This leisurely paced life, dictated by the seasons and ancient customs, was free from the oppressive, never-ending cycle of daily chores wives faced in the Pennsylvania colony from which Jemison had been abducted, not to mention men who treated their wives and daughters as little more than slaves and idiots.[62]

Furthermore, the depiction of the "medicine man" as a "superstitious dim-wit"[63] drew considerable criticism from First Nations individuals. One man called it "the basic stereotype about Native savagery."[64] Another wrote, "It just made me mad!"[65] A woman elaborated:

It seems like Hollywood always portrays whichever tribe they decide to pick on, in this case the Yuma, as evil. There is always an evil "medicine man" lurking around intent on killing or torturing someone and he is just as ready to victimize a member of his own tribe as a white person. The "medicine man" is always power hungry and he uses his mystic "evil powers" to intimidate or control others. This is a very white concept. The "medicine man" is not the Native version of the equally infamous "voodoo doctor." The real "medicine man" in our cultures is a person, male or female, who is a healer. Healers use herbs and other items provided in nature to treated the injured and heal the sick.[66]

As Tasiwoopa ápi has said,

Medicine People of any indigenous culture are typically chosen while still a child by a particular medicine society, usually clan oriented and at times with an animal as its base of strength and guidance. All of this said, "evil" or "bad" medicine is the antithesis of indigenous medicinal practice. The taboos or beliefs that are typically attached to the use of evil or bad medicine usually leaves the practitioner out of favor within the society they practice in and within the clan or tribal unit to which the practitioner was born into.

The USP (United States Pharmacopeia) was established using herbs and natural plants brought to the U.S. from Europe, Asia, and other parts of the world as immigrants arrived on this continent. The USP was greatly augmented by indigenous plants that traders and early explorers witnessed the indigenous peoples using to care for themselves medicinally. Many of these medicine societies survived the destruction and loss of their knowledge and ability to heal their fellow tribespeople. Many others have had to start from scratch and piece their medicine societies together from oral history. The bottom line is that medicine people and all of their training and practice leads them away from "evil" or "bad" medicine as they are taught only to use their knowledge to heal and perform ceremonies that will bring positive actions to the people.[67]

For another participant, "the visible use of a 'medicine man' that ended up being portrayed in a negative manner"[68] had another flaw: ". . . the fact that this scene with the 'medicine man' praying and conducting a tribal council was done during the day was ludicrous! This stuff usually took place during the evening, not during the daylight hours. Conducting discussions such as what to do with prisoners, praying to the 'Sun God' or whatever deity they were praying to, they usually didn't do things in the middle of the day when the sun was high. They would get up early and do things."[69]

The characterization of Natives performing human sacrifice also elicited a great deal of ire from participants. One woman disliked the portrayal of "Indians" as believing "that spirits come down from the sun . . . and are offered sacrifices," because "we don't do that."[70] "It's hard to believe that people would believe this crap,"[71] but "Indians sacrificing humans to pagan gods is a very old Hollywood stereotype that has been seen so often that way too many whites actually believe it is a part of Indian history in America."[72] "The sacrifice business, it's just wrong," pronounced another.[73] Additionally, "The Indians in this show are being portrayed as not advancing and staying the same . . . still wild savages getting ready to burn someone at the stake."[74]

The pseudo-ceremony performed by the "Indians" provoked a variety of commentary. "The typical showing of Indians dancing around in a circle which is usually seen on TV kind of still irritates me," stated one man.[75] "Give me a break with the silly dancing around the fire bit!" complained another.[76] "I was offended by the stereotypical 'Medicine Man' bopping around the fire like some primitive fool at a Halloween party,"[77] added a science fiction fan.

Comments such as "it makes me angry how all Native American Indians are made fun of in movies"[78] sometimes led to more blistering analysis: "Masks are ceremonial and sacred and should not be made fun of in this manner. Hollywood has no respect. Nor can they get past that stupid 'How! Me want 'um gold hair squaw' talk."[79] The following line is an example of that kind of speech:

INDIAN GUARD: Great Warrior Spirit come down from Sun. Where other paleface?

Comments such as "choppy English" and "I didn't like this clip because in it the natives spoke broken English"[80] occurred frequently in conjunction with more succinct complaints and criticism when participants listed the stereotypes they saw in the episode. A science fiction fan took Hollywood to task about it:

As a native speaker, I take exception to Hollywood "creating" "Indian speak," that wretched combination of broken English and grunts with gibberish that is supposed to pass for a native language. The tribes Hollywood refers to in this episode, the Yuma and the Comanche, are real. They have real languages, real customs, real traditions, and real people who did not vanish in the 1870s. Unlike this show, our songs are also real and have real, oftentimes sacred meaning. We aren't just buckskins and braids. We don't all just hop around a fire and live in teepees. Hollywood wouldn't dream of putting a Russian in Dutch wooden shoes, or have a devout Mennonite woman driving an SUV around LA in a miniskirt and five-inch high heels, or having an Asian speaking Yiddish. So why do they do equally outrageous things to Indian characters?[81]

This *My Favorite Martin* episode offered yet another example of the "all Indians live on one big reservation together" stereotype,[82] in which Hollywood has "all Indians dressing the same, as being the same, like using language as they please"[83] while they perform bizarre rituals. "I would not have them wear those headbands," one woman said disparagingly. "On every show we have seen, someone is wearing one."[84]

Many participants articulated concerns and criticism similar to this:

I dislike that [this] is another stereotypical use. We have the standard stereotypes—the Medicine Man with Central and Northern Plains headpiece, the chief with the full war bonnet and the lance with the supposed eagle feathers on it. There was the mix of clothing pieces which is typical. We had Comanche dress with full-length boots with winter leggings and winter tops. We had a typical drumbeat backdrop that was far too fast and we never saw the drummer. The typical dumb Indian who allowed his knife to be used to set the prisoners free. The writers chose these stereotypes because they didn't know any better. It has been their habit to mix and match outfits to fit their ideology to reinforce their habit to display the Indian as being the dumb boob, standing there scratching himself while his knife is being used to free the prisoner. Two final scenes of Indians and cavalry running headlong on each other rather than focusing on the escaped prisoners is typical foolhardiness of the cavalry and Indians in engaging one another. The last scene in Tim's house with the whipped Indian sitting on the horse is also very stereotypical. Once again the Indian loses and he got his butt kicked in the process. It did reinforce, in particular, Hollywood's version of Indians in their Laurel and Hardy kind of lifestyle in dealing with the dominant society. There were a bunch of little things—the intermix of different types of dress and clothing, different cultural iconography. They certainly weren't dressed up in all their stuff unless they were being pushed by the cavalry. And the language! They were clearly using a mixture of terms, mostly Oglala; they were [using] Lakota words for the Yuma.[85]

Nevertheless, mixed in with the negative comments were a few positive ones. While one man thought "this show looks like it was made for children,"[86] one woman decided it "was kind of OK."[87] "I liked the fact that it used some real Indians, which is odd enough," noted another man. "The medicine man was listed as Eddy Littlesky, but, of course, we don't know if he was Yuma or Seminole. The premise was okay for the timeframe, whites were being taking captive and marshals or sheriffs were constantly running them down."[88]

Additionally, some of the cultural imagery was correct. "The one thing I noticed that was positive was that all of the lodge doors were facing in the same direction."[89] Traditionally, Native lodges—in this instance, teepees—face east. This participant, however, went on to expose the flaw in this otherwise correct customary scene: "I believe the Yumas didn't use lodges; they were a Pueblo or Riparian people and would be living in hogans or something like that."[90]

All agreed that changes needed to be made in the way Hollywood portrayed "Indians" in science fiction. Many of the First Nations viewers agreed with how one woman said she would transform "Indian" stereotypes, were she writing this script: "I would change everything in *My Favorite Martian* from the dumbness of the Indians to the clothes they wore."[91] "I would be more Native sensitive," stated another.[92]

Others suggested that Hollywood take on the responsibility to be more accurate in its depictions of "Indians." As one woman wrote, "The Martian calls these Indians part of the Yuma tribe, but they are, in fact, [shown] living in teepees and wearing headdresses,"[93] which were not part of Yuma culture.

One participant saw the use of First Nations individuals to play the roles of "Indians" on the small screen as somewhat of a good idea gone bad: "While the actors are mostly Indians, they make Indians look stupid."[94] Another participant wrote: "I'm sorry the Native actor had such a lousy role, but at least Hollywood bothered to cast a Native in at least one part."[95]

One man talked about Hollywood's apathy when it came to accurate portrayals:

Nobody did any research. They didn't seem to care. Even the stereotypical treatment in the blonde's [Lorelei] lines, the word she used, the way the sheriff [Brennan] treated her later, was just yuck! Pick a culture, research it, make it historically correct dress, historically correct mannerisms, language. If you are going to pick the Yuma, use the right words, cast some Yumas. It's the complete failure on the part of the writers, scripters, and casters to portray or even make an effort to accurately show those whom they [Hollywood] chose to pick as characters. Allow Natives to use their language. There were speakers around. Get the clothing right. Historically and culturally it was completely inaccurate. The bottom line is that it was just a show that had Indians in it and the writers just didn't care.[96]

Nor did Hollywood writers, directors, and producers seem to care how inaccurately they portrayed First Nations peoples in more futuristic-oriented TV science fiction shows. Although First Nations peoples generally liked the idea that Hollywood would show them as alive and thriving a couple of centuries into the future, participants were not pleased with the way in which futuristic "Indians" were portrayed. One "trekkie" commented, "Unfortunately, *Star Trek* was very much a product of its time in many ways. It was Westerns in outer space, with whites civilized while Indians remained primitive throughout the centuries."[97] A variation on the comment that "movies and TV usually don't show Indians evolving disturbs me"[98] resurfaced repeatedly among participants—even among those who knew the progression of the *Star Trek* phenomena and its ramification for minorities on television. One First Nations "trekkie" explains:

Classic Trek had the ideas of a better humanity long before it was a national movement. It was also filled with '60s television camp and stereotypes. . . . In this episode, Native Americans from the "peaceful tribes" of Earth were transplanted to another planet, and then went about life waiting for a god from the stars to come to them. These Indians, now in the 23rd century, still looked and lived like those from the 18th—not one deerskin loincloth worth of evolution. And when did 18th-century Indian culture include gods from the stars? If this notion came as a result of being relocated, you would think that at least some evolution or technological advancement would have occurred, in the attempt to understand who or what moved them and where they now were.[99]

The portrayal of a lack of knowledge of basic survival skills also elicited many comments, such as the following example:

At first I decided the "Preservers" must have pulled a stunt like Kirk did in the fourth Trek movie *The Voyage Home*[100] when he "slingshot" the Klingon vessel around the Sun in order to go back in time to get the whales—only the "Preservers" got Indians instead of whales. How else could you find Native Americans running around in buckskins in the 23rd century? But even time travel can't explain away Miramanee knowing nothing of preserving food until Kirk teaches her! Where do you think jerky and popcorn came from? Our ancestors knew how to preserve food long before any white people showed up. That bizarre mixture of "peaceful tribes," who didn't all wear buckskins by the way, must have come from an equally bizarre parallel universe like in "Mirror, Mirror"[101] because people who don't know how to preserve food don't live long.[102]

Captain Kirk's rescue of the young boy received negative and positive comments. "When the captain was trying to help that little boy who was drowning, it kind of says that Indians aren't educated about saving lives in the twenty-third century,"[103] noted one woman. Another one added, "In this one Indians accept anyone as a god because he breathes the life into a little boy, so therefore he has magical powers!"[104] On a more positive note, one man commented, "I liked it when Capt. Kirk saved the Indian boy's life."[105]

The depiction of Kirk's arriving among the "simple savages who needed a 'civilized' white messiah"[106] to save them stirred up heated responses among participants. One participant thought the most negative kind of stereotype was exemplified "when Captain Kirk comes out of the temple [and] they [the 'Indians'] automatically worship him."[107] Another pointed out, "Why would they [Hollywood] think Indians would think another human could or would be a god? It's the old stereotype that white people are better than any other race."[108] Along similar lines, one man wrote, "Once again the white man thinks the Natives are too stupid to do anything. Since when has any Indian worshiped a white man as a god? The white man [is portrayed as] always saving the poor little Indian."[109]

Questioning the common sense of the *Enterprise*'s crew in the episode, participants mentioned the following sequence of dialogue when the landing party first spotted the village.

MCCOY: ... Shouldn't we contact them, Jim, tell them?
KIRK: Tell them what? That an asteroid is coming to smash their world into atoms?
SPOCK: They are too primitive to grasp the concept of space flight, doctor. Our appearance here would only serve to confuse and frighten them.

"One would assume that these Natives were transported to this planet in space ships, so why would the ever logical Spock assume the inhabitants couldn't understand the concept of space flight?" asked one woman.[110] Another added, "I didn't like it that they said we couldn't understand. They act like we're stupid."[111]

Participants overwhelmingly thought that the costuming of the "Indians" was "weird."[112] "The original *Star Trek* [TV series] was set in the 23rd century," observed one "trekkie," "so I find it ironic that the Star Fleet crew wear modern fabrics while the primitive Indians still run around in buckskins."[113] One woman commented, "It angers me to see people try to depict us to others on the television screen. What Navajos do you see wearing buckskin as everyday clothing?"[114] A man added, "I didn't like this because it showed a Native maiden in a mini-skirt."[115]

Putting the discussion into a more traditional perspective,[116] a woman contributed, "What does a head band have to do with medicine? Not just anyone can use medicine,"[117] and another commented, "How unoriginal is it to have all Natives dressing alike and speaking slow and simple talk. It's a stereotype to put us in teepees and war bonnets when whites people's clothing has changed."[118] Film director Stephan Feraca made a similar observation in 1964: "Now those movie Indians wearing all those feathers can't come out as human beings. They're not expected to come out as human beings because I think the American people do not regard them as wholly human. We must remember that many, many American children believe that feathers grow out of Indian heads."[119]

Beyond the clothing, many participants also questioned why were "only three tribes saved"[120] and "what's with Spock's pronouncement of these three 'more advanced and peaceful tribes?'"[121] Additionally, one participant was annoyed with "that silly tom-tom music in the background."[122] But that music is a Hollywood tradition that dates back to the silent-film era, when the "tom-tom beat, even when played on a Steinway, still means to most Americans that the Indians are on the warpath and trouble is brewing."[123]

Problems boiled over in the commentary following the showing of the *Star Trek: Voyager* episode "Tattoo" as well. One of the strongest stereotypical dilemmas Hollywood writers fell back on in this episode concerned generational conflict. One participant wanted to know why there is always "a wayward Indian child in denial of self"[124] in TV shows and movies about Indigenous peoples. Others voiced a more optimistic response. One participant wrote, "I liked that the episode showed how two generations can differ on cultural teachings (i.e., Chakotay's reluctance to accept his identity)," adding that "the impact of oral teachings" was also positive.[125] Another assessment, however, accentuates a problem many First Nations currently face:

One thing that I liked about the show and have seen in many families is the struggle between generations to keep the traditions alive, or in many cases learn those that have been lost. I have seen this in many forms—young people thinking that the old ways are useless. What I did not like was the fact that, considering the time represented and what is happening now in the present day, that drive to maintain the culture and traditions was not shown. It was saying that the will to keep alive the traditions was dead or dying and it took aliens to revive it. It gave the impression that all Indians, no matter what nation, were like that. Another problem I had was [that] these were supposed to be Indians—"Rubber [Tree] People"—how come there were no Indians there?[126]

The "no Indians there" aspect of this episode reaped even stronger criticism from another participant that was repeated in various forms by almost all of the participants:

The premise or story line proceeds well throughout the piece; however, shortly into the show it becomes evident that the producers have forgotten that Indigenous Peoples may be watching the show. The show's failure to cast Indigenous Peoples as "Indians" merely continues the ages-old mindset of refusing to employ Indigenous Peoples in their Traditional roles, guaranteeing them income, parity in their chosen fields of acting, and most importantly, giving Indigenous Peoples credence as Humans. Casting an Irishman (they are the only ones with alabaster skin, a translucency that is unmistakable), with long dark wavy hair as an Indigenous man alone is an insult, [and] as an Elder is a travesty.[127]

Still more negative comments on the episode deal directly with some of the centuries-old stereotypes: "children of the forest" and "viewed natives as being simple and wary of others";[128] "too primitive to have language or culture until whiteman came along and give it to us";[129] and "the placidness shown of a people . . . gave the impression that they were shy and all too soon trusting of another group of people . . . simply by knowing one word or one symbol they suddenly became brother of the skin."[130] Other participants listed stereotypes and comments in rapid succession:

(1) 'Tattoo' was typical of the movie media depiction of Indians being discovered. (2) Indians always primitive. White discoverers supposedly giving great things to the Indians (Sky Spirits, memory). Writers are ignorant and feed off of other uneducated writers and old movies. (3) Indians are the lesser people and there is this GREAT White Ruler. (4) Indians in show portrayed as ignorant and needing guidance. I really thought this show deserved ZEROs.[131]

And:

The stereotypes in the show were the same old ones. (1) Love and oneness with nature; [and] (2) the image of the shy savage hiding in the trees gazing at modern man are a few. This show showed how the dominant society overwhelmed another and its values replaced or destroyed what was before. It reinforced the image the dominant society has of Indians in that they were one with the land, and considered a simple group of people without the ability to achieve without the help of aliens from outer space.[132]

But amid all the negative feedback came a positive point of view:

One thing that was shown that I like about the show was that Indians had been on this land a long time. He [Sky Spirit] stated 45,000 years ago. When the time frame that places *Star Trek* in, I believe, the 2500s or more, that places Indians in the Americas way before Columbus's people even started to light their own fires.[133]

Another woman also mentioned Columbus, saying that she "saw the Sky Spirits from the Delta Quadrant as a metaphor for Columbus 'discovering' Indians and America."[134]

Others just shrugged at the episode and said they "thought it was a good idea to put an Indian in outer space"[135] and "well, at least we got an Indian aboard . . . [even though a] white woman always calls the shots."[136] A few held opposing views, insisting that "the Indian should not even be a part of *Star Trek: Voyager*"[137] and that "sticking an Indian on a spaceship crew is ridiculous because Indians aren't as curious about the unknown to decide to go into outer space and explore."[138]

When participants were asked if they would change one of the episodes' scripts, many cited the original *Star Trek* episode, saying that they would show the "Natives evolving over the course of time".[139] As one person put it, "In a futuristic show I wouldn't portray American Indians as savages, wearing buckskins and living in teepees, but how they really are."[140] All of those who wanted to see revisions to the *Star Trek: Voyager* episode would "have a real Indian guy"[141] on the series.

As a side note, *TV Guide,* in its special tribute issue to the thirty-fifth anniversary of *Star Trek,* listed "Tattoo" as number one of Chakotay's "Best Episodes."[142] The blurb characterized him as "proud and valiant, tracing his heritage back beyond the Mayans . . . unbending, but . . . capable of charm," although "spectacularly unlucky in love." Furthermore, the reviewer wrote, "His ancient lineage often manifests itself in surprising ways. . . . He proved to be a master carpenter. And he is said to give a great neck massage."[143] One can only speculate how Chakotay's being a member of the "ancient Rubber Tree tribe of Central America" makes him a "master carpenter" and handy-dandy with neck massages.[144]

Common Threads

"It's good to see Native Americans not only have a part in the future, but they can begin to shed some of the cultural baggage whites have saddled us with for so long,"[145] wrote one participant in summing up the episodes. Participants differed, however, when it came to their assessments of the generational conflicts portrayed in the *Star Trek: Voyager* episode. One participant highlighted both sides of First Nations peoples' differing opinions:

These shows made me sad, reminding me of all my people have lost due to forced or voluntary assimilation into white society. Our language, our traditions, our history, our stories, our identity, they have all been diminished because of assimilation policies dating back to the invasion. At the same time, and for once, these shows let TV viewers see the tip of the iceberg of problems currently facing Native Americans, especially about how to keep the traditions alive while living in [the] modern world around people who don't share and don't respect your beliefs.[146]

On the other hand, almost all of the participants disliked the depiction of "Indians" as "always primitive,"[147] "easily fooled,"[148] and "lesser people"[149] in "Go West, Young Martian, Go West, Part II" and "Tattoo," as well as "the white savior swooping down from the stars, saving the boy, the planet, and everybody but his own Indian wife"[150] in "The Paradise Syndrome." Several participants also found the acceptance of Kirk and Uncle Martin as gods by the "Indians" to be offensive and against Indigenous peoples' religious beliefs. Others loathed the way Hollywood depicted white control over Natives' lives. More of this will be discussed in the next chapter when Shoshones and non-Shoshones air their views on Hollywood's idea of modern Shoshones when a white man from the future leaps into a Shoshone's life in 1970.

CHAPTER 4

Shoshones and Non-Shoshones Assess *Quantum Leap* "Freedom"

A Special Showing

> *No group other than the Indian faces the precise situation in which their economic, political, and cultural fate is so completely in the hands of others. This is so because of the way in which substantial tribal resources are held "in trust," with management and regulation, if not always operation, resting with the federal government as "trustee." The result is that non-Indians in the Congress and in the executive branch control the fate of Indian peoples and their resources when they legislate and administer practices and policies.*
>
> *The media image is therefore an especially crucial and controlling one because it is that image which looms large as non-Indians decide the fate of Indian people.*
>
> —RENNARD STRICKLAND,
> *Tonto's Revenge*

A unique opportunity arose during the course of compiling information on First Nations individuals' view of Hollywood's "Indian" stereotyping of Shoshones in the science fiction series *Quantum Leap*. The show's "Indian" episode, entitled "Freedom," originally aired on NBC on 14 February 1990. In the episode, scientist, inventor, and time traveler Dr. Samuel Becket assumes the identity and the body of a Shoshone man during the year 1970.

Unlike television episodes such as *Superman* "Test of a Warrior," which names no specific Native nation, and *Star Trek* "The Paradise Syndrome," which identifies existing First Nations and attempts to blend together their cultures in Hollywood's version of anthropology, "Freedom" follows in the footsteps of the *My Favorite Martian* "Indian" episode, by directing viewers' attention to a particular tribe that was viable in 1970, 1990, and today.

None of the 17 women and 12 men in Survey Group 1 who viewed day-to-day depictions of broad-spectrum "Indian" lifeways and customs belonged to one of the Shoshone tribes. However, the occasion to show the *Quantum Leap* episode to 10 Shoshones—ranging in age from 18 to 46, with an average age of 22—arose in May and June of 2001. Of the 7 women and 3 men, 4 volunteered that they were science fiction fans. Their assessment of this episode, in comparison with that of the non-Shoshone viewers, offered some unique insights into how different First Nations cultures perceive stereotypes of one specific tribal society.

Quantum Leap "Freedom"

In the 1990 *Quantum Leap* episode entitled "Freedom," Sam Becket leaps into the life of a 25-year-old Shoshone man named George Washakie, the grandson of Joseph Washakie. The year is 1970—November 22, to be exact. At the time that Sam leaps into George's life, Sheriff Taggart and his deputy are beating up the young "Indian" man. The Nevada sheriff yells that it doesn't pay for an "Indian" to behave smart with him; then he and the deputy throw Sam in a jail cell with an older "Indian" man, who turns out to be George's grandfather. The sheriff says that Sam slipped. Joseph responds with "Looks like you slipped, too." Sam goes to the sink to wash up and sees his host body's reflected in the mirror, uttering his classic tag line "Oh boy," along with "I'm an Indian." Joseph laughs and reminds him that there are worse things—like being a white guy.

From Joseph, Sam learns that he "borrowed" a truck that reminds Joseph of a pinto pony he once had that was named Windwalker. When Sam points out that most people don't distinguish between theft and borrowing, Joseph replies, "Aw, primitive cultures." The elder decides they must break out of jail. When Sam wants to know how, Joseph snidely suggests that since Sam has lived in the city, he should be able to work out an escape all by himself.

Sam, as George, hides under one bunk, and Joseph sits on the other, singing. The sheriff comes in, wanting to know where George is. As expected, the sheriff opens the cell door and begins to look for George under the bunk. Joseph's song changes, alerting Sam, who punches the sheriff as he bends down. The two escape not fifteen minutes before Joseph's granddaughter Suzanne arrives at the jail. She wants Joseph returned to the nursing home. Taggart, preparing to pursue the escapees with a high-powered rifle, informs her that the old "Indian" is wanted for assault, theft, and escape from jail, and a nursing home is the one location where Joseph is not going to go when the sheriff finds him.

Meanwhile, Al, Sam's hologram helper and sidekick, arrives to tell

Sam he has leaped into George's life to help return Joseph to the Shoshone reservation so he can die where he was born. Al informs Sam that state officials and Joseph's granddaughter, Sam's sister, will not allow Joseph to return to the reservation. They fear he won't make the trip. Sam, who is a medical doctor in addition to being a scientist, decides he must take Joseph back to the nursing home, where he'll get the medical attention he needs so he will continue to live.

At that point, Al suggests that maybe just living isn't really enough of a reason. Joseph echoes this. But Sam, being insistent, suggests returning Joseph to the nursing home so that he can receive proper care while being near friends and family. Joseph reminds Sam that he moved to the city and that his sister Suzanne is busy with her own life. He gestures to the sky, the sun, the earth, and the wind, telling Sam that they are an old man's only friends. Sam points out that to live among such friends would bring about Joseph's death.

JOSEPH: My brother the hawk. All its life it flies where it wants, lights where it wants, loves where it wants. Now when it's near death, do you think it wants to be put in a cage? You've been too long among the white man.

Joseph goes back to the truck, and Sam argues with Al about taking Joseph where he can receive good medical care. Al reminds Sam that the sheriff is following them and that, by all appearances, greatly dislikes "Indians"; therefore, Joseph would not receive adequate care if he were captured. So Sam agrees to take Joseph back to the reservation.

Joseph wants to stop at a little gift shop on the way and get a buffalo hide, but he settles for an "Indian" blanket. Neither he nor Sam has any money. When Sam pulls out the pistol he took off the sheriff, the white store owner instantly assumes that Sam is going to rob him. Sam only wants to trade the gun for the blanket, an ancient Winchester rifle, and a bottle of oxygen for Joseph.

Joseph, deciding that the store owner has tried to cheat them because the gun was worth more than the exchange of goods, also takes a knife, which he gives Sam; a radio so he can listen to the football team that he considers the top in the country, the Washington Redskins; and some paint.

The old truck they "borrowed" happens to have a shortwave radio in it, and Suzanne uses the one in the sheriff's office to contact her grandfather, asking him to return. The sheriff cuts in from his vehicle, saying he'll get the judge to go easy on the escapees if they turn themselves in. Joseph responds to Suzanne by asking her to recall the last time any white person kept his promise to an "Indian." Had they taught her nothing in that fancy college she attended? He refuses to return just so he can "die like a worm in some white man's hut."

In order to get to the reservation over the mountain, they have to ditch the truck, which they "trade" for a couple of horses. They leave a note that says they will return the horses and that in the meantime the owners of the horses can use the truck as they please.

Joseph paints white dots on his face, which Al calls "society marks" when he explains the tradition to Sam. The elder then paints yellow hoofprints on his horse's neck to signify the number of horse raids he has made or the number of horses he has stolen. Al thinks it's terrific that they are witnessing the ways of the past. Joseph then makes yellow handprints on the horse's rump—one for each man killed in battle. Then he offers the paint to Sam, explaining that there was a look of one who had killed in battle about Sam's eyes. Sam puts two handprints on his horse. This is part of Sam's past seeping through that Joseph sees. Sam had, in previous leaps on the show, killed twice in order to save other people.

Just as they mount up, the sheriff shoots Sam, nicking a rib. Joseph returns fire with the Winchester, and he and Sam sneak off with the horses, as Joseph yells out, teasing Taggart that only whites shoot so poorly.

Higher up the mountain it's snowing. They seek shelter in a cave, and Joseph instructs Sam in how to build a small fire that won't be seen. But Sam doesn't have any matches. Joseph says he will show Sam an "old Indian trick" and starts to chant. Al gets all excited that they are going to witness this piece of Old West tradition. But Joseph strikes a lighter. Then Sam chides him about its being an authentic part of "Indian" culture.

Joseph's features soften as he begins to reminisce about how his son, the father of the "Indian" Sam leaped into, used to be fooled by his lighter trick time and time again. Joseph comments that Sam misses his father, and he wonders why Sam is so certain that his father is gone for good. Maybe that explains why Sam wants so desperately for Joseph to continue living. He explains that death is only a step in life, that people, like grasshoppers, simply discard one skin in death and hop into another, living a new life.

Skeptical, Sam questions the existence of another type of life beyond death's door.

JOSEPH: Then I would fight to hang on to this skin as hard as I could because it would be all I had. But it's not. All of life is a series of leaps for us grasshoppers. . . . Sometimes we see where we are going. Sometimes we don't . . .

AL: Is he talking to George or to you, Sam?

Sam and Joseph fool the sheriff by building a brighter fire and turning the radio on so that he hears voices; then they run off Taggart's horse and remount their own. At daybreak they have almost reached the river that marks the southern boundary of the reservation, but Joseph collapses before they reach the river and breaks his arm. Sam sets the arm, using a stick for a splint. He tells Joseph that there are so many things to learn that Joseph can teach him. Joseph responds that there is only one thing that needs to be learned, "that freedom is the greatest gift we're born with and the hardest thing to hold on to."

Suzanne rides up and begins to argue with Sam about taking Grandfather from the nursing home. Joseph points out that while the two young ones have been fighting, the sheriff just rode up over the hill. Joseph mutters that such in-fighting might well have been the reason that the "Indians" had failed to defeat the whites.

Sam tells Suzanne to get Grandfather over the river and onto the reservation, where the sheriff has no jurisdiction. Joseph wants to know if Sam plans to scalp Taggart. When Sam declines, Joseph thinks it's a pity, for the sheriff certainly deserves to be scalped.

Sam leaps on Taggart just as he takes a shot at Joseph. They fight, and Sam starts to scalp him. Al yells for Sam to stop. So Sam cuts off a piece of Taggart's hair. Taggart goes for his pistol and aims it at Sam. Joseph turns around and fires at Taggart. Taggart shoots Joseph.

Sam picks Joseph up and heads for the river. Taggart stops them.

SAM: All he wanted to do was die in peace, to die the way he wanted to. He didn't want to die inside a building surrounded by people he didn't know, hooked up to machines. He wanted to die surrounded by his friends. By the sky, by the wind, by the open spaces he grew up with. They were his family. They were his friends. All he wanted to do was die with dignity.

Sam starts crossing the river, Joseph in his arms. Taggart lowers his pistol. Joseph dies as they reach the reservation, thus providing another classic Hollywood "Indian" ending before Sam leaps into his next life.

Considerable literary license was taken by the writer, director, and producers of this episode in creating a type of "society markings" and symbols painted on the horses. In Shoshone traditions, "right angles or angular horseshoes represent horse tracks[;] . . . short lines, whether horizontal, curved, oblique, or vertical, indicate people killed by the wearer; broad painted bands record hand-to-hand encounters with the enemy."[1] Also, of the two military societies, the Logs were "honored for their military deeds, which entitled them to blacken their faces," whereas the Yellow Brows were "so named for their yellow painted cocks-comb hairdo."[2] None of these traditions matches what Joseph and Sam did in the episode. Thus the depiction of the horse stealing and painting, followed by the arrival of the hip-shooting Sheriff Taggart, ends up being the quintessential stereotype of playing "cowboys and Indians," although for "historical reality" Mihesuah suggests calling it "United States army and Indians."[3]

Nevertheless, during the five seasons of *Quantum Leap*, Sam "leapt" into a diverse variety of people's lives, crossing not only racial boundaries but sexual ones as well (and even species boundaries, as an "astrochimp" in Air Force training),[4] "seeing life through someone else's eyes," and grappling with social issues, "including racism, prejudice against the mentally handicapped, Vietnam, and the problems of single parents."[5] The "Freedom" episode represents the only time that Sam leaps into the life of a First Nations person, and the 1970 date is significant for Indigenous peoples in America because that was the emergence of the American Indian Movement (AIM).

On the other hand, had writer Chris Ruppenthal and the producers of this 1990 episode really wanted to expose America's anti-Indian sentiment during the 1970s, Sam would have leaped into an AIM member's life during the 1969–1971 occupation of Alcatraz Island; the 1972 Trail of Broken Treaties that led to the protest in Washington, D.C., and the takeover of the Bureau of Indian Affairs building; or Wounded Knee II in 1973.[6] Or Sam could have leaped into the life of an ordinary "Indian" living on the Pine Ridge Reservation during the 1975 shoot-out with the FBI or the "Reservation Murders."[7]

Instead, Ruppenthal writes Sam into the life of a Western Shoshone during the start of the U.S. attempt "to claim control over sovereign Western Shoshone land and people," beginning with the court battle between the Dann sisters and "public land" issues that date back to the federal government's failure to honor the 1863 Ruby Valley Treaty.[8] Ironically, these land issues, which have yet to be resolved, were not even touched on the "Freedom" episode.

First Nations Peoples' Assessment of the Stereotypical Depictions of Shoshones in "Freedom"

In the *Quantum Leap* "Freedom" episode, the standard Hollywood "warpath" consisted of Sam and a Nevada sheriff's duking it out in jail and, after Sam and Joseph escape, of their stealing a truck, a gun, and horses, thrown in for good measure. The stereotype of "Indians" being "warlike and treacherous" is "one of the most pervasive images of this country's native peoples" and educed strong responses from First Nations peoples.[9] "Even though many people in American society think Indians are not good people, Indians don't all steal," insisted one woman.[10] Another added, "I think this one [episode] says too much of Indians being worthless people, stealing/borrowing the truck, and escaping from the jail."[11] Other participants pointed out that in TV shows and movies "the Indian [is] always the thief and cheat,"[12] "Natives are in trouble" and "elder Natives [are shown] as wanting to die as warriors, no matter what cost,"[13] "Indians [are] always in jail or stealing, and breaking laws,"[14] and then "they always run and hide out on the rez."[15] In another participant's words, "America's picture of all Indians is negative."[16]

A Lakota man named Dan offers white author Kent Nerburn in *Neither Wolf nor Dog: On Forgotten Roads with an Indian Elder* a good explanation of the "Freedom" episode's aspect of "borrowing" versus "stealing" the truck and the horses. When Nerburn and Dan come across a child's bike left on a brushy hillside and Nerburn assumes that a child had lost it, Dan enlightens Nerburn on the "Indian" perspective:

White eyes, Nerburn. You've got white eyes. The boy probably left it there. This is what I mean. Watch our little children. They might get a bike and ride it, then just leave it somewhere, like that. You say they are irresponsible. They are just being like their ancestors who believed that you owned something only so long as you needed it. Then you passed it to someone else.[17]

On the other hand, the jail scene drew out many favorable comments regarding Joseph's use of what Joseph Marshall III calls "mystical and mysterious" abilities.[18] When Taggart realizes Sam is not in the cell, he demands to know how he got out. Very straight-faced, Joseph informs Taggart that Sam has become a raven and has flown away. Taggart, not buying it for a minute, demands to know why the old man hadn't done likewise. Again, very seriously, Joseph explains that he only has the ability to become a wolf and therefore he is too large to squeeze through the cell's bars. As one participant put it, Joseph and Sam "played off Taggart's notions about Indians in order to break out of jail."[19]

The white-to-"Indian" relationship, as exemplified by Taggart and Joseph, brought up the "only good Indian was a dead one"[20] mind-set, which remains a Hollywood devotion to an 1880s truism based on General Phillip Sheridan's "Indian policy" during his campaigns of the so-called Plains Indian Wars.[21] Sheridan's statement, told to a "friendly Indian," accurately "reflected a real attitude of the times, and it seems to be a latent sentiment that surfaces now and then" even today.[22] As one woman summed it up:

The fact that the sheriff hunted them [Joseph and Sam] relentlessly indicated the tendency of the dominant society to keep control of the Indians. The dominant society wants to tell Indians where to live and where to die. It was a classic display of the dominant white society of keeping Indians in a sub-class category of groups of people in the U.S. Sub-class meaning at the very bottom of the list.[23]

Another crucial issue brought out in this episode is the freedom to choose where to die. Comments on this issue ranged from "I liked how they showed the grandfather's feelings when he explained that he wanted to die surround[ed] by his culture instead of closed up inside some nursing home where the people couldn't understand the spiritual connection between nature and Indians"[24] to one that addressed this issue on a societal scale: "Today it is easy for us to put our elders in nursing homes. But they really don't see what happens in the homes. They don't get their meds, turned, bedsores, and they die alone."[25] Another participant saw the issue in the context of "Indian" stereotypes:

The story line was a quality effort to show the desire by many in the society to retain the right to die at "home." It was sadly the victim of a "cowboys and Indians" small truck chase complete with occasional stops for pistol and rifle firings. The only saving grace for this show is that the producers actually cast Indigenous People as such, all both of them. The fact that Scott Bakula is an Indian must be ignored, as he "plays" such an odd collection of different characters in the show that it has become the premise of the show. The writers and producers should have been the ones shot in the end for allowing the Elder to die especially so close to "home."[26]

Participants who had never seen this episode before were visibly upset as they watched Joseph being shot by Taggart and dying before reaching "home."

At the same time, participants couldn't completely dislike or disregard this episode. They each found positive things to balance the negatives. One woman admitted, "I liked Grandfather. He was portrayed well. He had strong beliefs, ideas, and was smart and humorous, and a real Indian,"[27] figuratively as well as literally. The *Quantum Leap* character Joseph Washakie is every bit the tongue-in-cheek spouter of what Vine Deloria, Jr., calls "cosmically comforting" Native wisdom, while at the same time offering "a fresh spin on the 'wise old Indian elder' stereotype."[28] Many participants enjoyed this flippant look at "the elderly being shown as the wise old sage"[29] full of "old Indian tricks,"[30] "because of Al and Sam's misunderstanding of the Native culture where Al was impressed with the 'mystic' teachings"[31]—a perfect example of what one participant calls "a Hollywood rarity of a show actually punctuated with ironic Indian humor, as well as real Indians wearing jeans instead of fringed buckskins!"[32]

Participants overwhelmingly enjoyed the humor in "Freedom," especially when it was essentially puns on "Indian" stereotypes such as when the show "used an Indian's 'super power' as a 'joke,'"[33] when Joseph "turned storyteller and fooled the sheriff with the Raven and Wolf story,"[34] and when "the Indian Grandfather always has a wisecrack or humorous remark."[35]

Indigenous viewers, however, were split in their observations concerning the episode's generation-to-generation conflict between grandfather and grandson. As Sam and Joseph reached the mountaintop and could see the river that formed the border of the reservation in the valley below, their dialogue exchange rings with the apprehensions of many First Nations peoples whose relatives survived "Indian" boarding schools that carried out the strict government assimilation policies.[36]

Joseph's hand sweeps the horizon, and he tells Sam that the "Indians" had lived free, wandering the plains and the mountains long before the invasion of the whites. The elders remembered this, but most of them had passed on, and too few of the younger people carried the memories of what the people had been and how they had lived. Sam then insists that it should be enough of a reason to fight for life, to live more years so the memories would be given to the next generation.

JOSEPH: No one wants to remember them. They have no heart for it. They are ashamed of what they are. They go to the city and take jobs in the factories or become schoolteachers [like Suzanne].
SAM: Maybe they are just searching for something. For themselves.
JOSEPH: They don't know who they are because they've forgotten who they are.

Some of the participants' comments about this segment echoed this one: "I like that they had the Indian in modern times and [he] still has his belief."[37] For others, this dialog brought a deeply emotional meaning to the surface, as eloquently explained by one participant:

This episode was good in that it showed the fact that many Indians have turned away from the old ways. Have in your famous words become assimilated into the dominant society. It was hard at times to watch the grandfather because I saw some of my own grandfather in him. He could not make my father understand the ways of our people, that our traditions, history, language and culture have to remain alive. It was good to see that the grandson began to realize the truth in his grandfather's words. It was never clear to me whether this clarity was true because the grandson began to understand, or whether Sam began to see the side of Indians that society had hidden from him. When[ever] I watched this show I usually got the feeling that Sam was on a path of learning with every leap he took and part of the people he touched remained with him, became a part of him in his journey.[38]

This same participant, however, also acknowledged that this is the "typical stereotype" of the "clash between young in one generation with the old—young Indians think that the ways of the elders are dead and they had to move on and fit into the white world."[39] Another pointed out that it was stereotypical that the episode "didn't have the young grandson portrayed as having a future or Native interest."[40]

Shoshones' Take on the Stereotypical Depictions of Shoshones in "Freedom"

Like other First Nations individuals, Shoshones took great exception to the episode's production team picturing Shoshone people as thieves and deviants. "Whites only see negative—everything we do is wrong,"[41] complained one science fiction fan. "I didn't like the stealing, then saying it was borrowing,"[42] stated another, a feeling that was echoed by others. "It isn't customary to have jailbreaks with Shoshone or Paiute people," insisted one man. Echoing this comment, a woman wrote that it was wrong to show "that Natives took things without asking and called it borrowing and/or even stolen."[43]

Although a fan decided that the stealing/borrowing "is not a stereotype—but can be assumed in that way,"[44] another expressed disappointment that Hollywood "decided to show Indians as fugitives, we live off the government, we're always in prison, steal, are stupid, etc."[45] One Shoshone woman, however, explained that Hollywood could not help but use old standard "Indian" stereotypes "because that's probably what they only know about Indians." She added, "They perceived Native Americans as bad people. [The production people] don't look at the good side of them [Natives]."[46]

Unlike the non-Shoshones surveyed, none of the Shoshones appreciated Joseph's "mystical and mysterious" abilities. Instead, they objected to the characterization that "Native Americans are mythical people."[47] They found the "wiseness and being honorable"[48] as stereotypical as the notions that "Indians are all traditional, spiritual, [and] wanted to be home"[49] on the reservations.

Further stereotypes that bothered Shoshones included "the image of oppressed people continu[ing] to live like they did before contact,"[50] the talk of "scalping that didn't come from Native Americans,"[51] and "war paint, face paint, feathers, Indian car, warriors, spiritual people."[52] One man declared that "they're stupid," referring to Hollywood writers, directors, and producers, because "they made it seem like all Natives have the same types of ceremonies."[53] "We all do not wear war paint. We have different Native cultures,"[54] stated another.

Inaccuracies such as the "feathers [and] war paint"[55] led to comments about other errors in Hollywood's interpretation of Shoshone culture. "I hate it when they use a different scenery for another tribe. The background or what is used for the Shoshone rez is not even what was filmed,"[56] criticized one woman. "The fact that they [Hollywood] had the traditions wrong"[57] upset another participant. Hollywood gave a "false impression of Native Americans (face paint, horses, etc.),"[58] affirmed another. One woman found the inaccuracy to be an ironic twist. "They do not know about Shoshones," she wrote. "They just know of what they heard or seen in movies."[59] "The ceremonial event of his [Joseph's] death needs more input or respect,"[60] pointed out another.

In comments of a similar nature, the Shoshones surveyed felt that the production team "made them Shoshone like how the white people see them as being. They only think of Indians dancing and doing crazy things—how they [whites] think we act."[61] Others shared opinions similar to that of a woman who wrote that writers, producers, and directors "are disrespectful because they put in the movie what they don't know."[62] Another suggested that Hollywood needed "to let people see that we're people and have feeling too!"[63] Unfortunately, as author Nancy Parezo has pointed out, "Stereotypes work best if there is little contact with, and actual knowledge about, the people categorized. In this way the categorizers do not have to deal with intra-cultural and intercultural diversity, which is messy."[64]

Alternatively, one man presented a uniquely Shoshone perspective when discussing the plot depiction of Shoshones defying the law and responding to the sheriff with violence: "The stereotypes of the white people are true to the treatment of Indian People, but there was no resistance in such a strong way."[65] Shoshone principal Chief Washakie strongly believed in and steadfastly maintained peace with the federal and other governments.[66] Furthermore, when Shoshones actually fought, they sided with the U.S. government and "were key parts of governmental campaigns against the Sioux, Cheyenne, and Arapaho."[67]

Additional negative comments focused on the Hollywood interpretation of the Shoshones' treatment of Native elders. A science fiction fan summed up the group's resentment: "Elders don't act like they are ignorant (reinforced primitive thinking towards Indians)."[68]

Paralleling other First Nations viewers, Shoshones also found fault with a story line that would put an elder in a nursing home. "Indian people don't place their elders in nursing homes,"[69] announced one Shoshone. Another proclaimed, "Our elders should not be placed in a white man institution. Leave them at their homeland."[70]

Shoshones also lacked enthusiasm with how Hollywood handled the "Indian" mascot issue. "What I didn't like about it [the episode] was how the old man kept talking about the Redskins, because that is degrading to Native American Indians."[71] Another found it stereotypical that an "Indian" would be fixated on "the football Redskins" team.[72] Mascots such as the Washington Redskins provide television viewers with some of the worst stereotyping, as Cornel Pewewardy has noted: "Indian mascots exhibit either idealized or comical facial features and 'Native' dress, ranging from body-length, feathered (usually turkey) headdresses to fake buckskin attire or skimpy loincloths. Some teams and their supporters sport counterfeit Indian paraphernalia, including foam tomahawks, feathers, face paints, and symbolic drums and pipes. They also use mock-Indian behaviors, such as the tomahawk chop, dances, chants, drum-beating, war-whooping, and symbolic scalping."[73] Unfortunately, the essence of such mascot and sports fan behaviors, dress, and mannerisms appears in the *Quantum Leap* "Freedom" episode.

In a different area, Shoshones held mixed views about Hollywood's idea of what Shoshone "Indian" humor should be. That Hollywood included Native humor in this episode struck the Shoshones as something of an oddity, seeing as how "Indians" supposedly have no sense of humor.[74] Devon A. Mihesuah accounted for this particular stereotype when she wrote, "Amongst themselves, Indians are talkative and jovial; they tease each other and tell jokes that would put *Evening at the Improv* guests to shame. Unless Indians feel comfortable around non-Indians or members of an alien tribe, the latter may never see their true personalities."[75]

One woman exemplified the duality of feelings when she wrote, "I like the humor of the elder. Native Americans are very humorous," adding, however, that not all "Natives are thieves and liars," as seen in conjunction with the humor in this episode.[76] In referring to the humor in the opening gambit where Sam realizes he has leaped into an "Indian" and Joseph informs him that it could be worse, he could be white, one participant commented, "It was okay . . . [the] 'white man say' part and sayings were funny."[77]

To the First Nations peoples of North America, the ability to make jokes about their situation became a survival mechanism. Mohawk actor Gary Farmer clarified:

Because Native communities have gone through probably the worst situations in North America that any peoples have gone through they had to have the ability to laugh. If they didn't, they wouldn't be existing today. So humour has been a means of survival, the only means. . . . For the last two hundred years they've had everything taken away from them, their ability to think, practically. Everything: what language they could speak, what religion they could do, and the things they couldn't do. It was all set out for them. They couldn't even make money in order to create a decent living for themselves. All those decisions were taken away from them. The only thing they had was their ability to continue to laugh their way through life because if they didn't . . . they would vanish.[78]

On the other hand, one Shoshone in the surveyed group best summed up the negative side of Hollywood's attempt at Shoshone "Indian" humor: "It was not so much the humor, just that it was stupid humor, like we're all supposed to be funny in every situation."[79]

On a positive note about Shoshones' take on Joseph and his proactive character, one woman elaborated: "I think I like the way the old man [Joseph] was persistent with wanting to pass away at home. He wanted to die as a warrior, the way he was supposed to leave his land. Back in the day [1970], or even now, we don't put our Native people in nursing homes."[80] Echoing this, a fan stated that she "liked the idea of the way he [Joseph] wanted to pass on, and talking about the old ways and warrior-like ways. I liked that he wanted to die in peace and the whole idea of trying to go back in old ways."[81]

Moreover, the positive commentary included the episode's attempt to portray Native life and efforts to retain or regain traditional culture in a modern setting. For example, one participant wrote, "What I liked about the story was the issue was about Native Indians."[82]

Although in all probability only a serendipitous plot device, one of the issues raised in the "Freedom" episode was unemployment on the reservation, which has reached as high as 70 percent and forced young Natives to leave the reservation in order to find work, but that doesn't mean they must forgo their customs, cultures, or traditions.[83] One woman found this episode a sad reminder that leaving the reservation does affect Natives' ability to maintain contact with their cultural and religious identities. "People don't want to forget their ways and/or not leave their ways to work in a factory or move off reservation for those reasons."[84]

Another issue in the episode dealt with the passing on of history, culture, and traditions through oral tradition. According to Mohawk author Beth Brant, "Oral tradition requires a telling and a listening that is intense, and intentional. Giving, receiving, giving—it makes a complete circle of indigenous truth . . . the power and gift of story, like oral tradition, to convey history, lessons, culture, and spirit."[85] Or as the Shoshones put it, as exemplified by one fan's response, "I liked him [Sam] helping the grandfather, learning from Elders."[86] (Non-Shoshone First Nations individuals mirrored this reaction.)

The only area in which the Shoshone audience survey differed from the general survey was the addition of one question structured to ascertain the measure of knowledge of Shoshone–U.S. government relations. The question was "Do you think there is anything significant about Sam leaping into a Shoshone man's life in the year 1970? If so, what?"

Only two Shoshones responded that the year held consequences for First Nations individuals and nations. One man described 1970 as a year in which white "people did not like AIM; Native causes; the struggles of reservation, government, lives," as well as the "different tribes" involved in the second "siege of Wounded Knee,"[87] which actually occurred during 1973.[88] The other respondent, a woman, described the year in more general terms, stating that "there was a lot of conflict between Native Americans and non-Native Americans."[89] Neither of these two Shoshones, however, addressed the problems specifically facing the Western Shoshones in 1970.

A third Shoshone stated that there was no significance to the year 1970, but she added "maybe the traditional beliefs of Natives,"[90] which were themselves under siege during the decade of the 1970s. The federal government, as well as the state governments, still arrested First Nations individuals for practicing their traditional religious beliefs prior as the passage of the Native American Religious Freedom Act which was passed by Congress in 1978.[91]

Unfortunately, these responses exemplify a huge problem within the First Nations of North America. Long before the days of "Indian" boarding schools such as the Carlisle Indian Industrial School and the Haskell Institute, established in the 1890s, the federal government began its eradication policy of First Nations history.[92] In 1791, President George Washington asked the new U.S. Congress to undertake civilizing "American Indians."[93] By the early 1800s, missionary schools supported by the U.S. government became the primary "educational institutions, instructing the Indian children not only in piety, but in traditional learning and in industrious work habits."[94] By 1849, Indian Commissioner Orlando Brown reported: "The dark clouds of ignorance and superstition in which these people have so long been enveloped seem at length in the case of many of them to be breaking away, and the light of Christianity and general knowledge to be drawing upon their moral and intellectual darkness."[95] Along with this "breaking away" from Native traditions came the destruction of cultural knowledge and history passed from generation to generation through oral tradition, which has left First Nations individuals in the "intellectual darkness" of not knowing their own peoples' history.

Furthermore, non-Natives possess even less information about the First Nations of North America and their contributions to American history. The only Shoshone history taught in schools across the country deals with Sacajawea's guiding Lewis and Clark across the West. Beyond that, Shoshones evaporated from the pages of history textbooks, just another tribe in the great unchanging American myth of the Vanishing Race. "We need to educate, and change the history books, too!"[96] affirmed one Shoshone woman.

Finally, paralleling the comments of other First Nations viewers, strong opinions flowed when the Shoshones discussed how they would change things in Hollywood if given the opportunity. One self-professed science fiction fan declared that the writers, directors, and producers should "learn more about the different tribes" and explore "different tribes' backgrounds . . . before making a movie."[97] One woman suggested an "all Native cast, crew and producers" be used,[98] like the one found in Sherman Alexie's *Smoke Signals*.[99] Others advised, "Make the Indians seem more real and not like the stereotypes"[100] and "show that Native Americans are individual people with unique cultures."[101]

One woman indicated that the experience of placing "the non-Native actor [Scott Bakula] in a situation that made him think of what Natives are faced with every day"[102] might help other non-Natives begin to see the amount and the magnitude of prejudgment that First Nations individuals cope with on a daily basis. Another participant suggested, "The Indian depiction can be switched around where we portray them [whites]."[103]

Common Threads

The First Nations participants of this study found some positives in the science fiction "Indian" images on television when they were used to debunk the standard stereotypes of the "stoic Indian," the "mystic Indian," the "wise old chief," and, in the case of the character Joseph Washakie, the wise elder whose "old Indian tricks" included things like cigarette lighters. One science fiction fan thought that the future provided the best option for demonstrating "the enduring presence of the original people on this continent."[104] Another expressed a similar sentiment:

Science Fiction shows and storylines that feature Natives can have a positive effect on Americans by not only presenting the fact that Natives continue to exist today, but that we will continue living tomorrow, despite what history books have told us for the last couple hundred years. We currently do and always have made contributions to the so-called greater society. If handled properly, Science Fiction can be a venue that begins the long and long-overdue process of correcting over five hundred years of erroneous stereotyping that we have to put up with on a daily basis. At least the *Quantum Leap* episode showed Natives dressed normal for the timeframe of 1970 and exposed some of the problems facing Natives as they try to reconcile traditional customs and culture with life in white America. Joseph's humor was also a decent start to showing Natives as more than stoic, cigar store Indians.[105]

Shoshones, however, generally found Hollywood's rendition of Shoshone humor less amusing than non-Shoshones did. Additionally, Shoshone participants watched the episode with a more critical eye when it came to the accuracy of Shoshone culture and the physical landscape that is so much a part of Shoshone participants' lives and spirit. First Nations peoples' views on Hollywood's versions of "Indian spirituality" will be explored in the next chapter.

CHAPTER 5

Sky Spirits in Space
"Indian" Spirituality and the Small Screen

> Each part of our religion has its power and its purpose.
> Each people has their own ways. You cannot mix
> these ways together, because each people's ways are
> balanced. Destroying balance is a disrespect.
> —MATTHEW KING, IN WARD CHURCHILL'S
> Fantasies of the Master Race

*I*ndigenous spirituality cannot be separated from the other aspects of First Nations peoples' daily lives.[1] Hollywood has not discovered that all episodes featuring "Indians" should also include spirituality. On the other hand, First Nations spiritual leaders are chosen by the elders and healers and must go through a long and difficult apprenticeship in order to learn how to maintain the balance of which Matthew King speaks.[2] This is not evidenced in Hollywood writers' idea of "Indian" religion.

This chapter examines the genre of TV science fiction in the context of how Hollywood writers, directors, and producers depict First Nations peoples according to Hollywood's interpretation of "Indian" spirituality. The first portion of this chapter consists of a synopsis and a textual analysis of an episode from three science fiction shows airing on television between 1954 and 1995. They offer classic examples of "the good, the bad, and the ugly" renditions (although not necessarily in that order) of "Indian" spirituality and religions found in science fiction TV shows. The episodes are arranged chronologically, starting with *The Adventures of Superman* "Test of a Warrior," which aired in 1954; *Star Trek: The Next Generation* "Journey's End," which aired in 1994; and *Star Trek: Voyager* "The Cloud," which aired in 1995. The second section of this chapter discusses how First Nations peoples view Hollywood's efforts to portray Indigenous religions in TV science fiction.

The Adventures of Superman "Test of a Warrior"

Scott B. Vickers could have been referring to "Test of a Warrior," a 1954 episode of *The Adventures of Superman* series, when he wrote, "The media continues to do its best to make the Indians the same and then to freeze them in the 'traditional times' of 1880s."[3] During the 1950s, when westerns ruled the airwaves, television primarily used period stories to showcase "red devil" images of "Indians." Science fiction, too, kept "Indians" frozen in the past, revealing little or nothing of First Nations peoples in step with modern times. A prime example of this pattern can be found in the "Test of a Warrior" episode.

Set in a time contemporary with its 1950s airdates, *The Adventures of Superman* generally revolved around the big-city problems of Metropolis.[4] Yet in the show's "American Indian" episode, Superman foils the evil "medicine man," Okatee, and his plot to keep Great Horse, the good would-be "chieftain" of an undesignated tribe, from assuming a leadership role.

Great Horse must suffer through the "ordeal" of the "tests of Donaga" in order to win the feather bonnet that would make him chief and that would make his own son Red Hawk the bona fide "medicine man" who will then succeed his father as chief one day. Okatee, the "treacherous" "medicine man," knows that Red Hawk refuses to practice "the old superstitions and fears" that the tribe's "medicine men" used against the people to keep them in line. Therefore, to bar Great Horse—and thus Red Hawk—from becoming the chief, Okatee sets up a series of tests impossible for a mere mortal to accomplish. Ironically, Red Hawk himself relies on a tribal "legend" and calls upon the "Great White Bird" (aka Superman) to help Great Horse pass the battery of tests, which includes surviving an attack by a "warrior" who wears bear-claw gloves and by chopping down a huge tree in a couple of minutes, both of which Superman surreptitiously accomplishes for the candidate. In the latter's case, Superman gets cameraman Jimmy Olsen to distract the warriors so that the superhuman can reach the tree and cut it unseen. The way Jimmy accomplishes this sets up the stereotypical tone of the entire episode:

JIMMY: Okatee, with this machine [camera] the paleface keeps records of important events. The medicine men of my people would be proud to have a picture of the brave ceremony of Donaga. There would be a picture for the wise Okatee to hang in his medicine lodge.

So, while Jimmy lines all the warriors up so that they are looking away from Great Horse and the tree and then blinds them with flashbulbs,

Superman hacks away at the tree until Great Horse's next blow with the ax-like "tomahawk" will topple it. Because Great Horse has completed all of the tasks, Okatee is disgraced.

The final trial is the "test of black smoke" (reminiscent of the "smoke signals" that Catholics still use to let the people know whether or not a new pope has been chosen). It involves the would-be chief's smoking a "peace pipe"[5] prepared by the "medicine man," Okatee. If white smoke comes out when the candidate puffs on the pipe, the individual becomes the chief. If black smoke arises, the individual dies, for the black smoke is laced with poison. All the warriors see Okatee add the poison to the bowl, so Red Hawk tries to stop Great Horse from smoking the pipe. Meanwhile, Superman's X-ray vision burns away the poison, and the smoke comes out white when Great Horse takes a puff of the pipe.

But when Red Hawk announces that the "Great White Bird has brought you a new chief," Okatee turns unbeliever and states that no such person exists and that Red Hawk speaks in the classic forked tongue to the tribal leaders. When Superman appears, Okatee says that it's a "paleface trick" and that the impostor must run the gauntlet unharmed to prove he is the "Great White Bird"—which he does. Foiled again, Okatee then reminds Great Horse of the legend of the "Great White Bird" and how the bird flew away into the sky. Okatee insists that the paleface must fly, since that is what the myth says the spirit can do. It is a test to prove that Superman is not the spirit. Of course, this is also accomplished with ease.

In the end, as a thank-you to Superman, Great Horse and Red Hawk go to Metropolis and give the newspaper editor Perry White (who wasn't even present at the ceremony) a chief's feather bonnet, reporter Lois Lane a necklace made from the bear-claw gloves, and cameraman Jimmy Olsen the "tomahawk" used to chop down the tree.

The blending of an actual First Nations religious object, the pipe, with made-up ceremonies such as the "test of black smoke" and the "tests of Donaga" started a precedent that would be followed in later TV science fiction, including *Star Trek: The Next Generation* "Journey's End" (vision quest) and *Star Trek: Voyager* "The Cloud" (medicine bundle and animal spirit guide).[6] With the symbolic trappings of a drum, a pipe, a feather fan, and a few "Indian" words, non-Natives can instantly be transformed, ignoring the fact that they are performing so-called "traditional ceremonies without any real knowledge or understanding of Indian ways."[7] The 1990s, with its disillusionment with white American culture, spawned intense curiosity about "tribal religions" and "the seemingly wholesale adoption of some of their ['Indian'] beliefs and practices by significant segments of white society."[8]

Although *The Adventures of Superman* was very much a show of the 1950s, when the norm for a woman character was the June Cleaver, *Leave It to Beaver* mom type, it's worth mentioning that since no First Nations female characters were present at or participated in the "test of black smoke" and the "tests of Donaga," the "Test of a Warrior" episode suggests that these were strictly men's ceremonies in a patriarchal society. Then why was Lois Lane allowed to view them? She may have been something of an oddity in a 1950s TV show, being a fearless reporter rather than a mom type, but she was still a woman at a men's ceremony. Even today there are ceremonies that are traditionally all male and ceremonies that are traditionally all female, just as there are certain protocols for each gender in joint ceremonies. My husband, Tasiwoopa ápi, while we attended a pow wow, prepared to take his place in the Grand Entry ceremony with the other Native veterans. He approached the flag bearers and the leadership of the veterans' group and asked for the honor of dancing behind all of the veterans and those who danced to honor veteran relatives, mostly women. Due to his status as a combat veteran, his request was honored, and he took the most rearward position among the veterans' contingent so that he might continue to serve as a warrior and protect those who danced in front of him. This responsibility belongs to the Warrior Societies and typically and uniquely to the Dog Soldier Societies.

Additionally, there is a noteworthy dichotomy in the names of the main "Indians" in this Superman episode. The "treacherous" "medicine man," Okatee, has an "Indian"-sounding name while Great Horse and Red Hawk, who are depicted as "progressive" and "good" because they seek to rise above the "old superstitions and fears" (become civilized), have translated names. Thus their very names serve as audio illustrations of the "good Indian" and "bad Indian" stereotypes.

Star Trek: The Next Generation "Journey's End"

Unlike *The Adventures of Superman* episode, which completely revolved around the "Indians" and their "medicine man" rituals, the "Indian" spirituality depicted in "Journey's End," a 1994 episode of *Star Trek: The Next Generation*, provides a subplot within a story line about a group of "North American Indians" who settled on Dorvan V, a now-disputed planet in the Demilitarized Zone recently established between the Federation and the Cardassians.

Captain Jean-Luc Picard of the Federation starship *Enterprise* has been ordered to remove, by any means necessary, the "Indians," whom Admiral Nechayev has characterized as a collective of nomads who decided to settle on the planet only some twenty years ago. When Picard suggests to the tribal council alternative planets with similar ecosystems located within the Federation territory, the leader Anthwara, in an effort to help the captain comprehend the importance of the new homeland, explains that environmental concerns were but a fraction of the reasons why the people settled on Dorvan V in the first place:

ANTHWARA: When I came here twenty years ago, I was welcomed by the mountains, the rivers, the sky.
OTHER COUNCIL MEMBER: Anthwara, he's laughing at you. He thinks you're talking about old superstition and nonsense.
PICARD: This is not true. I have the deepest respect for your beliefs. And the meaning they hold for your people.
ANTHWARA: Then you can respect the fact that this planet holds a deep spiritual significance for us. It has taken us two centuries to find this place. We do not want to spend another 200 years searching for what we already have.

Amid what becomes strained negotiations—with Anthwara at one point asking Picard about his family's history, because it is good to know about one's antagonist—the Cardassians attempt to take early possession of the planet, and the "Indians," descendants of the survivors of the 1680 Pueblo Revolt, refuse to acknowledge the validity of the treaty between the two superpowers. Meanwhile, an "Indian" named Lakanta seeks out Star Fleet Cadet Wesley Crusher, informing him that two years previously he, Lakanta, had entered the holy place known as the Habak, where he had had a vision quest. In it he had spoken with many different animals and spirits. He had also seen Wesley and knows that the cadet has come to this place seeking answers. When Lakanta takes Wesley into the sacred Habak, he wants to know about the figurines placed on the floor. Lakanta calls them "Mansara" and explains that the figurines symbolize the great variety of spirits that come to the sacred Habak. Wesley points to the one dressed like a Klingon, and Lakanta tells him about it.

LAKANTA: . . . our culture is rooted in the past, but it's not limited to the past. The spirits of the Klingon, the Vulcan, the Ferengi, come to us just as the bear and the coyote, the parrot.

Lakanta then tells Wesley to start the fire and wait for his vision quest to begin. In it, Wesley's deceased father, a Star Fleet officer, appears, instructing Wesley to follow his own path, not the one others expect him to take. Listening to the vision and knowing in his heart that it is what he should do for himself, Wesley resigns from Star Fleet in order to pursue his own destiny. He beams back to Dorvan V, where Lakanta divulges his true identity, that of the Traveler, an alien from Tau Ceti.[9]

Wesley assumes that the Traveler manipulated the vision quest and caused Wesley to see his father, but the Traveler insists that all he did was open Wesley's mind and that Wesley did the rest, by stepping outside the bounds of time and space.

TRAVELER: ... You've evolved to a new level. You're ready to explore places where thought and energy combine in ways you can't even imagine. And I will be your guide, if you'd like.

Meanwhile, Picard plans to remove the real "Indians" from the planet against their will, by beaming them up to the ship. Wesley warns them, and a skirmish ensues, complete with a phaser fight. Picard quickly persuades everyone to stand down before the incident escalates into war, and the "Indians" decide to give up their status as Federation citizens and to come under Cardassian jurisdiction in order to stay on the planet. Wesley also stays, for the alien Traveler has told Wesley that the "Indians" on this planet know much that Wesley needs to understand and he can learn much from them.

The "Indians" were not the only ones "aware" of things in this episode. The producers were attentive to the political correctness of hiring First Nations actors such as Tom Jackson (Lakanta) and Ned Romero (Anthwara) to play the "Indians." Ronald D. Moore, this episode's writer, was at least somewhat cognizant of Indigenous beliefs of the sacredness of everything and that the sacred is a part of every facet of the daily life of First Nations peoples.[10]

On the other hand, "Journey's End" showed no suggestion of the necessity of preparing for a vision quest.[11] Furthermore, Wesley undergoes the vision quest for personal reasons, rather than seeking specialized information through the means of a vision quest as a way to better serve the individual's community. Vine Deloria, Jr., explains this concept in the following manner:

Specialization occurs most frequently at vision quests or puberty ceremonies when young people sought help and guidance from birds, animals, and spirits. Often their careers would be shown to them and special information, roots, symbols, and powers given. This information would usually be shared with the spiritual leaders who had supervised the ceremony, but sometimes the person was told to bring a certain medicine, dance, or a bit of information to the rest of the community. The difference between non-Western and Western knowledge is that the knowledge is personal for non-Western peoples and impersonal for the Western scientist. Americans believe that anyone can use knowledge; for American Indians, only those people given the knowledge by other entities can use it properly.[12]

To prepare for his vision quest, Wesley does nothing more than transport down to the planet and enter a Habak, the "focal point" of the spiritual lives of the Dorvan V "Indians." In this episode, the Dorvan V "Indians" are said to be the descendants of Puebloan peoples. For Puebloan peoples, kivas are the "focal point" of their spiritual lives. In the show, the Habak structure is loosely based on a Pueblo kiva,[13] although unlike the kiva, which is a subterranean chamber, the Habak is not—Lakanta and Wesley climb up a ladder into it. Kivas—whether those in the ruins of Chaco Canyon or Bandelier in New Mexico or of Mesa Verde in Colorado, or modern kivas in use today in pueblos across the Southwest—are very sacred, very private places.[14]

Ironically, in June 1994 (three months after "Journey's End" premiered)[15] desperately-seeking-spirituality New Age "Indian" wannabes invaded a real kiva built by the Anasazis, located in Mesa Verde National Park.[16] The wannabe invaders "barred other visitors from the area while they performed chanting and drumming ceremonies."[17] This is the worst kind of disrespect of ancient and current religious beliefs, as well as the theft of First Nations religious and cultural traditions. To put it in Hollywood terms, this incident would be equivalent to the decision by the Nazi SS officers in the movie *Raiders of the Lost Ark* (1981) to commandeer Judaism and make it their own. As part of this seizure in the movie, the Nazis perform a "Jewish ritual" in order to safely open the Ark of the Covenant—except that, to be truly equivalent to the Mesa Verde incident, they would perform the ritual inside a Jewish synagogue in Jerusalem and they would not be annihilated by the "wrath of God," as depicted in the *Raiders* movie. Of course, anyone familiar with the story of the ark's power knows that only Jewish holy men were allowed to safely open the ark. All others were destroyed, and Hollywood respected this spiritual story in its portrayal of the holy relic in the *Raiders* movie.

At the fifth annual meeting of the Traditional Elders Circle, held in 1980 in the Northern Cheyenne Nation, traditional elders from diverse First Nations drew up a resolution, in part warning that the spiritual hucksters of Indigenous religious ceremonies should be aware that their inappropriate and illegal use of Native American religious ceremonies and artifacts would be "harmful to the individual carrying false messages" (the non-Native huckster) and to those who paid these unqualified people in order to participate in ceremonies sacred to First Nations peoples. The elders' purpose in making the resolution was "so that no harm may come to people through ignorance and misuse of these powerful forces," which Indigenous religious leaders spend years learning "before ceremonies and healing can be done."[18] Still, Hollywood writers and others continue to disrespect First Nations spiritual stories and traditions in movies and on television.

Star Trek: Voyager "The Cloud"

Episode six of *Star Trek: Voyager* (1995), "The Cloud" provides a perfect example of what Vickers calls "the 'my man Friday' syndrome," in which an "Indian" is characterized as a "subservient yet honorable character, capable of assisting the dominant culture in the fulfillment of its destiny."[19] "The Cloud" is also the first episode of this television series to mention anything about Chakotay's mystic spirituality,[20] which is so incidental to the plot that it doesn't even rate a mention in the "official" episode guide synopsis.[21]

As a bit of background, Chakotay had quit Star Fleet and joined the resistance group known as the Maquis after Cardassians killed his father. The Maquis were fighting both the Cardassians and the Federation to preserve their people's home world, located in the Demilitarized Zone.[22] In the midst of a battle between the Maquis and Star Fleet, Chakotay and his crew get hijacked by an alien and dumped in the Delta Quadrant, along with the Star Fleet crew on board *Voyager*. Stuck 70,000 light-years from the Alpha Quadrant and home, the two crews have been forced to band together in order to survive in the completely unexplored and unknown section of space.

As a result of homesickness, morale ebbs, and Captain Janeway hopes that the discovery of a nebula—which turns out to be a life-form that *Voyager* first injures and then heals—will cheer everyone up, for there is no counselor on board. In a conversation conducted over the opening credits of this episode, Chakotay tells the captain that when his people need a counselor, they communicate with animals: "It's a Native American tradition."

Taken slightly aback, Captain Janeway wants to learn more. So Chakotay explains that animal guides choose to accompany humans through life and that this phenomenon is similar to Carl Jung's 1932 innovation concerning an "active imagination technique." Of course, Native peoples have been accomplishing the same sort of animal-human communication phenomenon many centuries prior to Jung's idea, with every person having his or her own animal spirit guide.

Later in the episode, Chakotay produces his medicine bundle and uses it to introduce Janeway to her personal animal spirit guide. The whole thing is an aside that serves no real function in this episode. Chakotay was to use his akoonah—a high-tech device that his peoples' scientists developed to facilitate vision quests without the use of traditional "psychoactive herbs" and that he keeps in his medicine bundle—in two other episodes,[23] but neither searching for nor receiving counsel from an animal spirit guide nor the power of his medicine bundle received any further attention in the show's seven-year run.

The use of the medicine bundle to search for an animal spirit guide in "The Cloud" suggests "Plains Indian" origins, as evidenced in the discussion about animal guides between the captain and her "Indian" first officer.

JANEWAY: . . . Yours is a bear. . . . You strike me as the bear type.
CHAKOTAY: Thank you. The bear is a very powerful animal. It has great *pejata*. But he's not my animal guide. The creature that guides us doesn't define who we are. It merely chooses to be with us.
JANEWAY: Okay, if not a bear, then what?
CHAKOTAY: I can't tell you that. It would offend my animal guide if I spoke its name . . .
JANEWAY: . . . Can one just chose their own animal guide?
CHAKOTAY: . . . If you're interested, I'll be glad to teach you how to contact your animal guide.

"Pejata" means "medicine" in the Lakota language.[24] It is also "a common substitute word for peyote among Native American Church folks and, especially, in the Sioux medicine songs."[25] This, coupled with using the medicine bundle to search for an animal spirit guide, sets up a contradiction with "Tattoo," the second-season episode that features Chakotay's tribal background. In "Tattoo," as noted in chapter 3, Chakotay's people are depicted as descendants of "(pre)Mayans" living in the Central American rain forest.

Another inconsistency shown in "The Cloud" deals with Chakotay's spirituality as portrayed within this one episode. He does say in the aforementioned dialogue that animal spirit guides become offended if one were to talk openly about them; however, he ignores proper treatment of medicine bundles. Of course, there are an amazing number of books on bookstore shelves that describe "Native American religion" and "Indian spirituality" in great detail, sprinkled with ethnographic and historic accounts to make them "authentic."[26] The majority are written by Euro-Americans or Europeans and contain inaccurate and inappropriate information. Nevertheless, since the show's writers, Tom Szollosi and Michael Piller, present aspects of actual Indigenous religions, they could have attempted to respect First Nations peoples' religions in their depiction.

For example, Kiowa author N. Scott Momaday wrote a tasteful representation of a medicine bundle in his novel *Ancient Child*. Momaday alluded to the power and purpose of the medicine bundle as his character participated in traditional life, but he never actually described its contents or how it was used, for to write about these things would be improper in traditional First Nations societies.[27]

First Nations Peoples' Assessment of "Indian" Spirituality as Depicted in Science Fiction TV Shows

In the stereotyping of First Nations spirituality by Hollywood writers, the First Nations observer of Hollywood's programming realizes that these writers have not consulted First Nations peoples about spirituality. So what do First Nations peoples think about these stereotypical portrayals? What would they do differently, were they given the opportunity to write a TV script dealing with First Nations religious beliefs? The participants in this study had plenty to say.

Receiving remarks such as "it was stupid"[28] and "really hokey,"[29] *The Adventures of Superman* episode "Test of a Warrior" garnered the most commentary, not because of its 1950s look or special effects but for a variety of other reasons, the main one being the completely irreverent way in which Red Hawk treated his elders and especially his and his father's attitude toward the "medicine man," Okatee. This irreverent portrayal offended several participants. "To my people, spirituality cannot be separated from all the other aspects of our lives," explained one woman, "as well as part of identification of our clans, our respect for our elders, our medicine people, and our traditions."[30] Another elaborated on this same concept by writing, "It makes our religion look foolish and childish. The mocking of Native religion bothers me because we take our religion very serious."[31]

The pipe is a sacred object for the majority of First Nations peoples. Many members of the survey group found the way Hollywood represented the sacred pipe in "Test of a Warrior," as illustrated in the following exchange, to be insulting.

RED HAWK: Pipe of black smoke means death if the medicine man is displeased. And Okatee is angry. . . . Okatee will fill the pipe. My father will smoke it. If the gods will it, the legend says he will live. But if Okatee is against Great Horse becoming chief . . . (After filling the pipe with tobacco, everyone sees Okatee adding powder from a different pouch.) That black power is a poison . . . I'm sure of it. I won't let my father smoke it . . .

GREAT HORSE: My son, if I have not the courage to complete Donaga, tell me, can a man live without honor? Could I ever again face my people? Or you?

OKATEE: . . . Great Spirit, touch the pipe to be smoked. Let the lips of the warrior Great Horse bring him life or death. Donaga.

One participant explained why this scene upset her so much:

When our people were forcibly removed from their homelands, the whites stripped our people of everything they could, including the majority of our sacred objects, which are now in the possession of private collectors and museums. But some of our spiritual leaders managed to safeguard some of our most precious sacred objects, including a pipe that had been used in our ceremonies since before whites began tampering with our society and our sacred ways. I can't begin to describe just how angry the Superman clip made me when the "evil medicine man" tried to kill the warrior by putting poison in the ceremonial pipe.[32]

Another participant elaborated, insisting, "Although many things in the Superman episode bothered me, the one that most disturbed and offended me was that the so-called medicine man used a sacred pipe as an instrument for murder."[33] In a related comment, one man discussed the sacred pipe: "The 'peace pipe' is a common stereotype [and] with all that smoking and abuse of tobacco we'd have all died of lung cancer years ago. Tobacco was used, not abused. Native American spirituality has too much respect than to be an 'abusive culture.'"[34]

A couple of participants mentioned that the episode was "somewhat amusing."[35] One person wrote, "It was hard to take it seriously. The Great White Bird statement was the most humorous."[36] But most participants disliked the tendency to portray Superman (aka the Great White Bird), with Jimmy as an accomplice, as the "saviors of the poor, dumb Indians."[37] The "whites came to save the day,"[38] explained one man. Another said that the episode presented an attitude of "white is saver/helper,"[39] when Great Horse rolls his eyes skyward and pronounces, upon successfully completing Donaga and assuming the role of chief, "Warriors of the past, gods, and Great Spirit, peace and plenty must be ours, for the Great White Bird [in the form of Superman] has come amongst us, and he has blessed us."

One participant summed up the episode as "completely unrealistic": "Superman saves the day. All would go to hell if there wasn't someone to take care of the Indians."[40] Another woman objected to "showing traditional ways as 'heathen' . . . childish and simple-minded": "Apparently Superman is the Great White Bird, showing White people as godlike or protector father-figures to Native Americans."[41] Yet another participant added, "Overall, I disliked how the whites were condescending and superior to the Natives." She elaborated: "The white people looked superior because they 'knew better' than the superstitions the Natives 'supposedly' believed. The Natives looked foolish because they were duped by Superman's powers to rid the pipe of the poisoned smoke."[42] One woman commented negatively that "the white man was shown as all-knowing and wise."[43]

In conjunction with this "white superior/Indian inferior" depiction,[44] participants overwhelmingly remarked on the "broken English"[45] spoken by the "Indians" in the episode. "Have Indians talk in their real voices instead of Hollywood stereotype 'Indian sound,'"[46] insisted one woman. "It's a 'Hollywood thing,' the only portrayal society knows,"[47] explained another. Additionally, the "Indians" are shown as "understanding the English language but unable to speak it."[48]

Furthermore, participants expressed anger over the way the "Indians" were dressed in the *Adventures of Superman* episode. Just as in the wretched nursery rhyme, ten "Indians" parade around the set of "Test of a Warrior," costumed in Hollywood's idea of "Plains Indians." Their clothing consists of fringed and beaded buckskin shirts in some rather wild designs, beaded leggings, breechcloths, moccasins or boots, and full feather "headdresses"[49]—except for the two who wore feathers reminiscent of very stylized Haudenosaunee headdresses and Okatee, who wore a buffalo horn headdress with the horns pointing forward in a rather demonic fashion.

More than one participant echoed this comment: "The costumes bothered me. They were a tribe of leaders as represented in dress and no followers."[50] Or as another participant explained it, "Very typical war bonnets for everyone!"[51] One man found the dress the most stereotypical image in the episode "because it portrayed Indians as if they were still a part of the past."[52] The wearing of full headdresses and "Indian buckskins" by the "Indians," while the whites wore modern clothing, also brought out comments such as "they made the Indians seem stupid . . . the war paint, feathers, customs, passing around the peace pipe";[53] "Indians appear to not exist in contemporary times, leading contemporary lives";[54] and "the 'progressive' Indian views ancient religion as superstitions used to control the people: very offensive!"[55]

Moreover, the war paint drew much criticism. "All the warriors watching this ridiculous test sported war paint over their already very heavily made-up faces,"[56] observed one participant. Another looked at the importance of and meaning behind wearing war paint in his culture: "Getting painted had spiritual significance. Everything we did was done for a respectful purpose, not for the hell of it."[57]

The set for the episode also received censure: "The style of dress was Plains, but the background was rocky-cliff-like with trees. Supposed to be the Black Hills?? . . . The whole thing reminds me of a Boy Scout camp and people trying to talk like the Natives."[58]

On the other hand, viewers' observations of the *Star Trek: The Next Generation* episode "Journey's End" differed greatly from those of the *Adventures of Superman* episode, based on whether the participants held traditional beliefs[59] or practiced Judeo-Christian teachings in addition to traditional beliefs.[60] The majority of those participants who classified themselves as Judeo-Christian, as well as following the traditional spiritual beliefs of their tribe, disliked the way "Journey's End" depicted the sacredness of everything, for the same reasons those who practiced only First Nations traditional religious beliefs liked the spiritual depiction of this episode the most.

One participant disliked everything about the episode, including "the way the Indians talked" and "addressing the 'vision quest.'"[61] "The whole vision quest thing, sending Wesley out for his vision, the whole concept is crazy," wrote one woman as an explanation of why she disliked the episode.[62] Echoing this, another said the episode bothered him because "to the Indians everything was sacred."[63] These participants referred to the following portion of dialogue in "Journey's End":

LAKANTA: Habak is holy to us. We hold our rituals and our ceremonies there. It's sacred to us. What's sacred to you?

WESLEY: ... I don't know ... I have a lot of respect for things. But I don't really consider anything sacred.

LAKANTA: ... Everything is sacred to us. The buildings. The food. The sky. The dirt beneath your feet. And you. Whether you believe in your spirit or not, we believe in it. You are a sacred person here ... you must treat yourself with respect. To do otherwise is to desecrate something that is holy ... perhaps it's time for your own vision quest to begin.

Among those survey participants who keep only traditional religious beliefs, comments tended to follow along the lines of this example: "I liked this one. It was real, not all fake. The stereotypes were not so much stereotypes but real Indian beliefs. It was also good 'cause it told how sacred the land is to Indians."[64] Or as another put it, "the belief in the sacredness of all things and all that is around us is more in keeping with our traditions."[65] As traditional participants saw this episode, the story followed Susan Berry Brill de Ramirez's explanation of the sacred among cultures with strong oral traditions. She wrote that "the sacred is manifested in the relationships between each person and all other parts of creation."[66]

The episode's portrayal of Wesley, the white Star Fleet cadet, as taking part in a vision quest also received diverse comments from traditional and Christianized participants. One person was not comfortable with Wesley's being considered "chosen/special."[67] Another elaborated on this opinion: "I did not like how there were connotations of Wesley Crusher seemingly acknowledged as superior so he was worthy of finding his own spiritual journey with Native guidance."[68]

On the other hand, one participant explained why she found this episode appealing: "One thing that I like was the fact that this episode showed the relationship of all things. And in Wesley Crusher's case of his part is one thing that I like in some ways because it reminds me of what I went through after heart surgery . . . and my visitor . . . a [traditional] holy man who prayed for me and with me and helped me find the path that brought me here."[69] Another participant liked that "the young man who is seeking the reason for his life" realized that "the material, educated way is not enough for his spiritual being."[70]

Captain Picard also drew both negative and positive remarks. One participant found it a very negative image that he was sent to the planet to be the "savior/advocate" of the "Indians."[71] Another wrote that the show "makes [the] elder look bad when he remembers the horrors of the past. Capt. [Picard] tries to justify that he had no association with past wrongs and that they should be forgotten."[72] Another honed in on Picard and a flaw in the history: "I did not like the way they showed Picard as the savior they [the 'Indians'] were waiting for. Partly because Picard is French and the people that attacked the Pueblos in the 1600s were Spanish. They [the writers/producers] needed to get their history right. The French were in Canada and Louisiana, not New Mexico. If I had written the episode I would have shown more of the cultural strength of the Pueblo elder in resolving issues of their people."[73]

Others applauded the inclusion of actual history in the story. As one man pointed out, "*Star Trek: The Next Generation* was one of the better shows that showed and told Native history such as the Pueblo Revolt."[74] Another commented, "It's like history repeating. Forced removal of the Natives from their homes." The same participant added, "The only good thing in any of the videos was in the second one ['Journey's End'] when the elder was talking. There were some words of wisdom—'We know that nothing that happens is truly random'—and a short history lesson."[75] What's more, one individual added that she liked the fact that the writers depicted the "Pueblo tribe not Plains Indians"[76] for a change.

Nevertheless, one survey participant found nothing positive in the scene with "the Native Aliens around a table talking about things that are real in a fictional form," adding, "That isn't right."[77] Another woman wondered, "Why can't t.v./movie Indians ever use contractions?! . . . [I] did not like the stoic, deeply serious personae. No sense of humor!"[78] Additionally, "How come all aliens in *Star Trek [The Next Generation]* are fluent in English, but the Native Americans are stilted?"[79]

Furthermore, Lakanta, the "Indian" who opened the door to Wesley's vision quest, received disapproval for being "a little bit too dramatic about Indian spirituality"[80] and because of "the idea of the Native spiritual guide who wasn't even Native—he was an alien instead."[81] She explained: "I think the stereotype of Native shape shifters[82] was extended to the Native man [Lakanta] who ended up being the white time traveler. This was a flagrant disrespect of being Native by [depicting that] even the true identity of the Native man was changed into something he was not—a superimposed white (yet alien) time traveler."[83]

Traditional participants who commented on the episodes' lack of respect to First Nations religious beliefs took a slightly different approach to the *Star Trek: Voyager* clip, which included Chakotay's use of the medicine bundle, a sacred item among First Nations cultures that have medicine bundles. In the scene, Chakotay enters the captain's Ready Room (office), carrying a folded-up deerskin, which is his medicine bundle.

CHAKOTAY: ... I've never shown it to anyone before. After what you said this morning I thought that it was important to let you see.
JANEWAY: Will it help me find my animal guide?
CHAKOTAY: Eventually you'll have to assemble your own medicine bundle. But this will allow me to assist you in [your] quest for a guide ... (He sits on the floor at a low table and unfolds the deerskin, spreading it out into a square. Janeway sits down beside him. He holds up each item as he tells her what it is.) ... A blackbird's wing; a stone from the river, and an akoonah ... my ancestors used psychoactive herbs to assist their vision quests. Now they're no longer necessary. Our scientists have found more modern ways to facilitate the search for animal guides. Place your hand on it and concentrate on the stone. A-koo-chee-moya, we are far from the sacred places of our grandfathers. We are far from the bones of our people. But perhaps there's one powerful being who will embrace this woman and give her the answers she seeks.

Regardless of whether they held traditional or traditional and Judeo-Christian beliefs, participants found this episode offensive for its "superficial view of Indian spirituality."[84] Those following traditional beliefs echoed this individual's objections: "This entire episode bothered me because a medicine bundle is sacred and is never opened or shared with anyone."[85] "You don't just show up at somebody's office and unwrap sacred objects *without any preparation on anybody's part!* Medicine bundles contain sacred ceremonial objects that must be handled in an appropriate manner at all times,"[86] insisted another. Or as one man explained: "Chakotay's medicine bundle was his, not hers [Janeway's]. It was a personal medicine bundle. Had he been taught properly or had he paid attention to his father or elders' teachings, Janeway, as a woman, would have never seen his medicine bundle. They are not related. There is no connection other than she is his commander and it does not apply in this context. Unrelated individuals, male or female, rarely, if ever, see, let alone handle, someone else's medicine bundle."[87] Nor was the captain's office an appropriate place for a vision quest, as one man pointed out in reference to the interruption of Janeway's journey into "Indian" spirituality: " 'Vision quest'—'spirit helper'—I'm sorry. I should have closed down my computer before the vision quest. Ha! That was a good one!"[88]

Others who held Judeo-Christian beliefs protested the pseudo-magical content of the scene in the captain's office: "Chakotay unwrapped a medicine bundle and acted very mysterious. I didn't like how Janeway seemed mysteriously transfixed by the lizard. The writers were drawing on the concept that Natives were spiritual and looked to animal guides and the bones of their ancestors. This is a common stereotype today, also spirit guides that would talk to you through an animal. What I disliked the most was Janeway almost kissing the lizard to hear it 'speak' to her. The whole thing seemed surreal and hokey."[89]

Many survey participants remarked on the "influence of New Age spirituality"[90] on the show. The " 'Indian spirituality' seems more like an Eastern yoga exercise,"[91] wrote one individual. Another insisted, "Wow, if only we could find our guides so easily!! I wish I could have a spiritual quest so easily. Then again they have made Tarot cards with a Native theme—Sweatlodge Cards, Animals, Medicine Women, etc." This "only adds to the New Age bullshit,"[92] one woman concluded. "The episode totally falsified the finding of animal spirits," another woman wrote, adding, "It is not what I went through to find/meet mine. Then again I am not of the 'Rubber Tree People' transported from the Artic to Central America by Aliens from space!"[93] Or as one person summarized: "Everybody can be Indian! Just get an animal guide!"[94]

Furthermore, some of the participants found Chakotay's dialogue to be of the stereotypical stoic variety—"stilted speech, always sermonizing,"[95] as one woman characterized it. On the positive side, this same participant found "some humor"[96] in the episode. Another was thankful that "Janeway's spirit guide was a lizard and not a bear, eagle, etc."[97] Others mentioned comments similar to this one: Chakotay's "one with nature [was] better only because he's dressed like everyone else, so he's not stereotyped in buckskins [therefore he's] not seen as much as an 'other.' "[98]

Common Threads

Participants in the survey groups found it disturbing that Hollywood writers appear to consistently rely on stereotypes when parading "Indians" across the television screen, even in outer space and centuries into the future. But considering that these stereotypes have been around for centuries already, it shouldn't come as a surprise that Hollywood continues to project them into the future.

Additionally, First Nations peoples found the dichotomy between the two *Star Trek* series' portrayals of First Nations spirituality both interesting and sad—interesting in that they are so different, even though they were only a year apart, and sad in that the producers didn't follow through with the respect shown in "Journey's End" in the creation of Chakotay and his groundbreaking role on *Star Trek: Voyager*. One participant offered this insight: "Overall I think those shows with an Indian theme—story lines—are just the start of what could be shown. I also see and understand why actual ceremonies will never be shown. It takes from the sacredness and could trivialize the ceremonies. No TV/Media episode could actually depict the feelings one experiences going through them."[99]

For participants, *Star Trek: The Next Generation* really was the pinnacle of decent treatment of First Nations religious beliefs in the *Star Trek* universe and beyond. To First Nations peoples, this doesn't appear to bode well for the future of "Indians" in television. Although the following First Nations participant was speaking about the *Star Trek: Voyager* series, his response sums up First Nations participants' views of "Indian" spirituality as seen in TV science fiction: "The producers, knowing that this show was set 300 or so years in the future, probably decided to take some liberties based on assumptions that things would change over that period of time. Well, at least they didn't make it all up, but perhaps it would have been better if they had rather than piece him [Chakotay] together from several different cultures."[100]

Concern about the homogenized nature of the "Indian" tribes in the TV science fiction episodes viewed is but one of the participants' comment areas examined in chapter 6.

CHAPTER 6

Visions for the Future

*A*s stated in the introduction, the purpose of this project is to explore participation responses of First Nations peoples to "Indian" stereotypes portrayed within the TV science fiction genre, as represented in the seven episodes examined in this project, with the expressed focus of giving voice to First Nations peoples' reactions to these stereotypes.

A stereotype that First Nations peoples experience all too often (although not one portrayed in the TV episodes viewed in this project) is that they are not intelligent enough to articulate their concerns themselves; their words are not eloquent or sophisticated enough to be put before the general public.[1] The stereotype is that "Indian" words require translation into appropriate academic language by non-Native experts who understand "Indians" better than they understand themselves.[2] Or as one survey participant put it: "What I really despise are Anglo-European teachers/educators who still have a sense of paternalistic ownership of everything that is indigenous because they are experts and therefore they know more about us than we do ourselves because their 'his story' lessons are a major contribution to the continued racism that American Indian people face. 'Their story' is not even 1/8 of the truth because they have written junky stories to flatter themselves and to demonize us."[3]

As was discussed in chapter 1, the survey questions were designed to be open-ended or nonleading so that participants were free to write about their own experiences and lives, rather than attempting to read the researchers' goals by reviewing the questions. Not all of the participants have been quoted. Some took the opportunity offered in the survey to address issues that were not related to the project, while comments of some others were too similar to those already quoted. In those cases, the commentary that most clearly expressed the participants' perspective on the topic was quoted.

Analysis of Common Threads: Positive and Negative Comments on Stereotypical Depictions of "Indians" in the Science Fiction TV Episodes

There were a total of 682 comments on the stereotypical depictions of "Indians" shown in the science fiction episodes: 539 negative, 141 positive, and 2 on the significance to the year 1970 (plus 3 on no significance to the year 1970).[4] The comment area that received the most negative responses was the lack of respect for elders, traditions, and religious beliefs (with a total of 63). The comment area that received the most positive responses was how the "Journey's End" episode of *Star Trek: The Next Generation* depicted the traditional First Nations' belief that everything is sacred (15 responses). *Star Trek: The Next Generation* received the most positive comments (49) and was the only episode for which the positive and negative comment areas tied, with each side receiving 6 areas. For all the other episodes the negative comment areas outweighed the positive areas. The *Adventures of Superman* "Test of a Warrior" and *Star Trek* "The Paradise Syndrome" tied receiving approximately ten times as many negative comment areas than positive ones, with 15 negative to 1 positive for *Superman* and 11 negative to 1 positive for *Star Trek*. *My Favorite Martian* "Go West, Young Martian, Go West, Part II" received 18 negative areas to 3 positive areas. See appendices E and F for further details.

Four of the episodes elicited contradictory comment areas among the participants. Regarding *Star Trek* "The Paradise Syndrome," 1 participant liked that Kirk saved the "Indian" boy, whereas 11 didn't like Kirk's being portrayed as the white savior of the "Indians" and 9 disliked his being worshipped as a god. (After Kirk administered CPR and saved the boy's life, the chief announced that only a god could bring the dead back to life.)

With regard to the *Quantum Leap* "Freedom" episode, 10 participants in Survey Group 1 commented that it was good that the grandson realized the importance of elders/traditions/culture, while 2 responded that the grandson was depicted as having no future or Native interest. This latter comment might have stemmed from the episode's establishing that the grandson had left the reservation at age 14 and had not returned for over a decade, as well as his having a factory job in the city that evidently didn't pay well enough for him to own a car. At the opening of the episode, grandson and grandfather had been jailed for stealing a truck. As the story progressed, Sam got more into the role of the "Indian" grandson and began to understand the importance of traditional knowledge, as well as realizing that it was in danger of dying out with the elders.

The Shoshone Survey Groups also expressed contradictory commentary about the *Quantum Leap* "Freedom" episode. Two liked the episode's "Indian" humor, while 4 thought the humor was "stupid."

In *Star Trek: The Next Generation* "Journey's End," the dichotomy was very clear-cut. Fifteen participants liked that the episode made everything sacred, while 7 responded that they disliked that the episode made everything sacred. This split in opinion appears to have depended on whether or not the participants held only traditional First Nations religious beliefs or also held Judeo-Christian beliefs.

In the *Star Trek: Voyager* "Tattoo" episode, 9 participants commented that they liked the episode's (and the series's) portrayal of "Indians" in outer space, while 1 participant disliked the depiction of "Indians" in outer space. This latter participant cited a lack of curiosity about the unknown as the reason for this response.[5] It is not known whether this participant was raised with or exposed to traditional beliefs. Generally speaking, First Nations peoples who are raised in a traditional manner learn to closely observe the world around them in order to know and understand it. Therefore, nature (their surroundings, regardless of where they are) are not part of the Unknown. Also, the Native worldview describes First Nations peoples' place in the universe and with all those who inhabit the universe. This view is quite different from the scientific worldview, which seeks only to explain the universe itself as well as the dominant society's steadfast need to control the unknown and the universe.

Participant Reactions While Viewing the Episodes

Participants often scowled and many made low grumbling or hissing sounds or otherwise expressed displeasure during the viewing of *The Adventures of Superman* "Test of a Warrior." This episode is a product of the 1950s—when movies, movie newsreels, and television all portrayed "Indian" religious beliefs as the superstitions of still-primitive people[6]—but, as one participant wrote following the viewing, "In the episode the representation of religious beliefs was made fun of and made to look like the believers of the Indian faith can easily be fooled."[7]

There was also a wave of agitated movement, angry expressions, and groans or growls when Okatee used the pipe, a sacred object used in prayer in the majority of First Nations peoples' religious practices, for evil and harmful ways. There were mutterings when Red Hawk and Great Horse called upon the "Great White Bird" (Superman) for help, as well as when Jimmy distracted the "Indians" by taking their picture.

While viewing the *My Favorite Martian* episode, angry movement occurred during all scenes with the Yuma camp and the "medicine man." Participants uttered clearly perturbed sounds when the "Sun God" appeared to collect his sacrifices, and they grumbled over the warrior's use of "broken English." The dialogue with the word "squaw" set off distressed movement and hissed comments.

Participants offered audible sounds of dismay and disbelief over Spock's pronouncements about the mixture of the three peaceful tribes and how simpleminded they were in *Star Trek* "The Paradise Syndrome," as well as the chief's verdict that Kirk was a god and deserved the "medicine badge." Additionally, there were a few giggles when Miramanee first appeared.

Laughter punctuated the viewing of *Quantum Leap* "Freedom" by Survey Group I, especially when Joseph observed that the deputy resembled a sheep, tricked the sheriff into coming into the jail cell, and performed the "old Indian trick" with the lighter. There were a few snickers when Joseph said that the Redskins[8] were the "best damn team in America" and he loved it when they beat the Cowboys. On the other hand, when the sheriff shot and killed Joseph in the end, participants were openly upset. There were gasps, stunned expressions, and distressed murmurings, followed by total silence.

When Shoshones viewed *Quantum Leap* "Freedom," they did not laugh at Joseph's humor. The Shoshones fidgeted in their seats during the jailbreak, the theft of items, and the application of the so-called warrior markings to the horses. Although no outward expression was shown when the sheriff shot and killed Joseph, there was a period of total silence at the end of the viewing, followed by several moments of inactivity before participants filled out their surveys.

Other than giving either approving or disapproving nods when Lakanta discussed what was sacred in *Star Trek: The Next Generation* "Journey's End" and making a few disapproving sounds when Lakanta turned into the Traveler, the viewers remained quiet.

There was no outward reaction to *Star Trek: Voyager* "The Cloud," other than some agitated movement when Chakotay brought his medicine bundle to Captain Janeway's office and they immediately began her "vision quest."

General displeasure was expressed through murmurings and agitated movement when the hawk attacked Neelix and when the alien explained how his people had given language and culture to Chakotay's ancestors in *Star Trek: Voyager* "Tattoo."

Common Threads in the *Star Trek* Universe

With regard to both episodes involving Chakotay on the *Star Trek: Voyager* series, the "Indian" crew member received negative comments that ranged from vexation to outright anger from First Nations participants in both survey groups—from his lack of respect for elders, traditions, and religious beliefs, his offensive use of sacred objects, and his assimilation into the dominant society (giving up his "Indianness") to his being non-Native playing a Native character. These negative comment areas for "The Cloud" and "Tattoo" received a total of 59 comments out of 102 negative responses for these two episodes shown. To the majority of participants, including all but one of the First Nations "trekkies," Chakotay embodied a whole sequence of "Indian" stereotypes. One fan illustrated:

Chakotay is the quintessential Tonto in outer space and that disturbs me. He follows Janeway around like a well-trained dog. Other than a couple of times when he used his medicine bundle and that stupid so-called personal medicine wheel to help other crew members, his Indianness vanishes just like most whites think all Indians have vanished into white culture or just died out altogether. He even told B'Elanna that her visions of her mother on the Klingon Barge of the Dead were just hallucinations caused by a head injury and to just forget about them.[9] No Native person would ever dismiss another's visions as hallucinations or tell them to ignore their religious beliefs. And what's with all that stuff about those Sky Spirits being Delta Quadrant aliens who "gave" Natives language and culture! That says Natives would have remained primitive children of nature who respected the land but couldn't communicate with it or each other or show the land their respect because they had no language or culture until a more civilized, advanced race came across the vast ocean of space to help Natives progress. Gee, it's a good thing the Delta Quadrant aliens didn't follow Star Fleet's Prime Directive any better than Captain Kirk did; otherwise Chakotay would never have been smart enough to get into Star Fleet![10] It's sad that he, the only Native role model on TV, is such a poor representation of Native culture and spiritual practices. Despite what I guess were good intentions to put a Native on a Star Trek crew, [Rick] Berman[11] really did a good job of massacring Native culture and spirituality on Voyager.[12]

Other First Nations "trekkies" eyed the stereotyping of Chakotay from different angles. One woman admitted, "I have always been disappointed in the character of Chakotay. To me he is just another assimilated Star Trek officer. There is nothing of his traditions that he brings to the forefront in any given situation."[13] Another looked behind the scenes for the source of the show's "Native American" character: "I think the only reason Berman put a Native American character in the crew was that it was the PC thing to do about the time the series started. But he didn't even bother to get a REAL Native person to play the part! How politically incorrect can you get! Kind of defeats the purpose of Chakotay in the first place, doesn't it?"[14] Opposing this view was this one:

I like that the character of Commander Chakotay is a 24th-century Native American shown in a positive way. Although he is played by an Hispanic actor, Chakotay is an integral part of the crew and could be seen as a role model. While *Star Trek* is science fiction, it strives to promote racial and cultural tolerance as an established fact of humanity's future. ... I will admit that I am a fan of *Star Trek*—despite some of the early camp, and I also enjoy the character of Chakotay, played by Robert Beltran. But it would have been more in the spirit of *Star Trek* to actually cast a Native American to play a Native American. After all, any other racial group plays characters of their race, Black, White, Asian, etc.[15]

Another First Nations "trekkie" commented on the multicultural-ism of the *Star Trek* universe: "I like *Star Trek*. It's a science fiction show that has many different type[s] of creatures that live on different planets."[16]

On the other hand, First Nations peoples practicing traditional re-ligions agreed that *Star Trek: The Next Generation* "Journey's End" represents the genre's best attempt to demonstrate "Indian" spiritual-ity on any of the episodes. Five of the 6 positive comment areas dealt with aspects of "Indian" spirituality and culture, receiving 43 of the episode's 49 total positive comments.

Common Threads in "Indian" Spirituality

Negative and positive comments about "Indian" religions, customs, traditions, and origins transcended the *Star Trek* universe and included *The Adventures of Superman* "Test of a Warrior," *My Favorite Martian* "Go West, Young Martian, Go West, Part II," and *Quantum Leap* "Freedom" as well. On the negative side, comment areas about the de-piction of white society and white religion as superior to "Indian" spiri-tual beliefs and of "Indian" religious beliefs shown as foolish received a total of 78 comments in the seven episodes. "The sad depiction [in the episodes] offers only stereotypes" that the dominant society continues to use in illustrating "Indian" spirituality, which is also depicted as "expendable or like you can pick one up like a magazine or at the 7-11," one woman wrote, adding "No respect. It makes me sad and MAD!"[17] Another woman elaborated on this: "The federal government, the same one that reminds us every Thanksgiving how the brave Pilgrims suf-fered all those hardships in order to have religious freedom, have forced their religion on us and constantly tell us we worshipped the wrong god."[18] Others added that "white society thinks we don't have a god or that we dance around a fire worshipping the Devil"[19] and that the dominant society depicts First Nations peoples as "only communing with or praying to nature, plants, animals, rocks, spirits, anything and everything but the Creator."[20] Insisted another, "I think they are afraid of our religious beliefs because we take part in sweats and dance as part of our religious practices."[21] Another participant put it this way: "The dominant society has little or no concept of Native American religions. They are too hung up on having control over everything in nature, having the world revolving around them. Our religious beliefs are just some New Age fad they are trying out like the latest diet or fashion. They can't begin to truly comprehend our spiritual beliefs. They don't even want to. It's just something different to try until something else comes along."[22]

Other Common Threads

The comment categories of "Indians" being frozen in time and being part of a homogenized tribe received a total of 62 comments from participants after they viewed *The Adventures of Superman* "Test of a Warrior," *My Favorite Martian* "Go West, Young Martian, Go West, Part II," *Star Trek* "The Paradise Syndrome," *Quantum Leap* "Freedom," and *Star Trek: Voyager* "Tattoo." Taking on a persona to match the stereotypical "Indians" in the comment areas, one First Nations woman summed up:

I think the stereotype that bothers me the most is that there is such a thing as an Indian. I have no problem being called "Indian" or using the term either. It was good enough for Mom, ya know. But what it is that ticks me off is that all our diversity gets conflated—we all lived in teepees, ya know, and we all hunted bison/buffalo. And hey, didn't the nations who did those things also make pots (which they packed up on their ponies when they moved from place to place, 'cause no one farmed either, ya know), and carve totem poles (which they also drug behind their ponies, and planted when they stopped) and ocean going canoes. Ain't we all matri-patri-lineal, and we all have dark red skin and long black hair, and brown eyes, and we all talk about the Great Spirit 'cause we all believe the same thing, eh? And we all speak the same language, too. Well, except there are two different tribes, right? Plains and Southwest, right? And the rest of us don't know anything 'bout nuttin'—at least that's how it'd seem if you believed the stereotype.[23]

The white savior was another stereotype that provoked some heated commentary. This comment area, along with the "Indians" needing whites' help or guidance, and whites giving culture and language to "Indians" received a total of 27 comments from participants after viewing *The Adventures of Superman* "Test of a Warrior," *Star Trek* "The Paradise Syndrome," *Star Trek: The Next Generation* "Journey's End," and *Star Trek: Voyager* "Tattoo." With the exception of Captain Kirk's saving the "Indians" from planetwide annihilation in the original *Star Trek* and Captain Picard's saving the "Indians" from being forcibly removed from Dorvan V, the "white" saviors to which the participants referred were supposedly aliens—Superman from Krypton, the "Sky Spirits" from the Delta Quadrant, and, as mentioned in 4 other participants' comments, the "Indian" who turned into the Traveler from Tau Ceti in *Star Trek: The Next Generation* "Journey's End." All of these aliens were played by white actors, but so were many of the "Indians." The key to why these participants saw these alien characters as whites might lie in one First Nations woman's comment that she "saw the Sky Spirits from the Delta Quadrant as a metaphor for Columbus's 'discovering' Indians and America."[24] These "white" aliens were depicted in a manner consistent with 500 years' worth of European and Euro-American behavior toward "Indians." Superman saved the good "Indians" from their own bad/evil "medicine man." The Traveler knew and disseminated "Indian" culture to the white youth Wesley. The "Sky Spirits" brought language, culture, and progress to the "primitive" "Indians."

An alternative explanation offered by another participant, based on "the idea of the Native spiritual guide who wasn't even Native—he was an alien instead," bears repeating. She defended her stance: "I think the stereotype of Native shape shifters was extended to the Native man [Lakanta] who ended up being the white time traveler. This was a flagrant disrespect of being Native by even the true identity of the Native man was changed into something he was not—a superimposed white (yet alien) time traveler."[25] The root of objections to Lakanta's transformation into the alien Traveler may be found in attitudes that First Nations people have toward colonization, which has been trying to superimpose white culture, customs, belief systems, religion, language, and lifestyles on First Nations peoples since contact.

An alien, a Martian in the case of *My Favorite Martian*, pretending to be the "Sun God" of the Yuma Nation also disturbed First Nations individuals, as reflected by a science fiction fan's comment: "Some writer in Hollywood specifically chose to name the Yumas as the villains in this episode. They created a mishmash of culture, clothing, and created bogus ceremonies and that wretched Sun God, then, to add insult to injury, [they] have a white guy/alien impersonate this supposed god. While this is offensive under any circumstances, it is even more so because the Yumas are a real people with a real culture and a real religion. None of it resembles this Hollywood farce."[26] Another participant wrote:

What is particularly sad about all the circumstances in the preceding paragraphs [commentary on the episode] is that Hollywood, in its halfhearted attempt to become politically correct when portraying Indigenous North Americans, is that they have created a situation that is, in fact, worse than what they were doing before. Their underlying critical failure is to involve members of those sovereign nations that they [Hollywood] openingly choose to name in their episodes, in this case the Yuma, while giving absolutely no credence to the sovereignty to the individuals involved and the socio-cultural difference of the individual sovereign nations. Their continued failure to employ Indigenous actors to represent their own tribes or simply to represent Native actors, instead choosing to use dark-skinned Caucasians, continues to be the ultimate insult and travesty.[27]

The Yumas were but one of six actual sovereign nations named in the science fiction "Indian" episodes in this study. Unfortunately, unlike the Shoshones watching a supposed Shoshone episode, no Yumas were among the survey groups to give an added element of commentary about their own culture.

The Depiction of Shoshones on *Quantum Leap* "Freedom"

Non-Shoshones viewing the *Quantum Leap* episode "Freedom" defined 8 positive comment areas and only 9 negative areas, whereas Shoshones found only 4 positive areas and 14 negative areas. Overall, Shoshones were more focused on the inaccuracies with their own culture than were non-Shoshone viewers, who could not be as attuned to Shoshone traditions, customs, and culture. Likewise, Shoshones found fault with the setting and the insinuations that Shoshones did not know their own culture or care enough to want to learn it.

Both Shoshones and non-Shoshones failed to appreciate the depiction of Shoshones as thieves and criminals, escaping to the rez. Both groups complained about the incorrectness of an elder's being forced to live in a nursing home and a granddaughter's insistence that her grandfather return to such an institution. All expressed concern about how the "Indians" in the episode were maligned; however, for the Shoshones the concern was from the standpoint of Hollywood's negative portrayal of their culture and people. Non-Shoshones conveyed more criticism over Hollywood clichés and white assimilation attitudes.

Finally, the humor that received 9 positive comments with non-Shoshones only garnered 2 positive comments from Shoshones, while 4 other Shoshones insisted that the episode's humor was stupid.

What First Nations Peoples Would Like to See

As one First Nations science fiction fan commented: "At least somebody in America is willing to admit we survived all the dominant society's termination and assimilation policies and that we will continue to exist in the future—even if Hollywood is only showing this picture through science fiction."[28]

Of course, one could argue that because science fiction, by its very nature, is plainly labeled as fiction, the viewing public would realize the fictitious nature of the "Indian" spirituality and futuristic lifestyles portrayed in the episodes. Hollywood writers, directors, and producers, however, have (mis)represented actual aspects of First Nations' religious ideas, ceremonies, and sacred objects. One First Nations "trekkie" gives producers the benefit of the doubt, "based on assumptions that things would change" by the time frame of any futuristic shows. But this participant also suggests that it might be better to "make it all up" than to assemble First Nations traditions, customs, and lifeways piecemeal into "Indians" of the homogenized tribe.[29]

On the other hand, many First Nations elders and leaders have expressed anger over the growing number of non-Native (and unqualified Native) practitioners of ceremonies supposedly " 'based on' Indian traditions" and the outright theft of traditional religious practices.[30] Continuing to depict inaccurate portrayals of First Nations customs and religious beliefs on television could be seen as being in these categories, even though the shows are fiction.

Given that viewers tend to believe that what they see on television (and in the movies) is an accurate representation of First Nations peoples, lifeways, and religious beliefs, then the dilemma becomes whether or not to show any First Nations traditional customs and religious beliefs and, if so, what and how much to show.[31] First Nations participants who hold traditional beliefs want to see Hollywood "get rid of the superior viewpoint of the whites and make the part about the Native Americans more realistic with respect for their personhood and beliefs"[32] in its portrayals and to present more tribal diversity than "Plains Indians practicing Southwestern and factious[33] religions".[34] They would also like to see Hollywood not depicting "whites as the gods or saviors of the Indians,"[35] not making light "of how animal spirits are found, as they are our protectors, guides and teachers,"[36] as well as showing "Natives as a regular, equal part in the world and time in which they live"[37] in the overall society. One science fiction fan suggested "consulting the elders of the tribe being shown or whose ceremonies are being shown," and then to "go with what they say."[38]

Unfortunately, with Hollywood's crank-it-out attitude, it is unlikely that writers or producers would take the time to seek and obtain the approval of tribal elders before depicting "Indian" ceremonies and traditions in a television show or would change the depiction if the elders asked that their ceremonies NOT be accurately represented. As First Nations actor and activist Russell Means has pointed out, "Our religions are *ours*. Period. We have very strong reasons for keeping certain things private, whether you [the non-Native public] understand them or not."[39]

Conclusion and Epilogue

*O*ver five hundred years have passed since Columbus "discovered" the First Nations peoples of the Americas, but the stereotypes generated in the media in the wake of his "discovery" continue to be used and to be believed by television viewers. This is quite obvious in such productions as *Star Trek: Voyager*. The writers, directors, and producers of the series didn't consult First Nations peoples when creating a "Native American" crew member who, whether Robert Beltran wants to admit it or not, is a role model for First Nations young people.[1]

If, however, the writers, directors, and producers in Hollywood listen to First Nations voices, "Indian" episodes should and will be written and acted by First Nations peoples, with tribal elders being consulted on content. This might put an end to the two major negative comment areas participants had about the episodes—the lack of respect for elders, traditions, and First Nations religious beliefs shown by Hollywood writers, directors, and producers; and the offensive depiction of the use of sacred objects. The third major negative comment—the inequity between the seemingly "superior" or "civilized" dominant-society culture and the perceived "inferior" or "primitive" "Indian" culture—might also be alleviated.

On the positive side, participants' major comment areas were specific to two of the episodes: *Quantum Leap* "Freedom" and *Star Trek: The Next Generation* "Journey's End." The non-Shoshones enjoyed the depiction of Joseph in *Quantum Leap* "Freedom" as a wise grandfather who behaves like a real "Indian" grandfather; how his grandson comes to realize the importance of elders, traditions, and culture; and the humor shown in the episode—all of which are a real leap away from the "Indian" stereotypes. Participants also appreciated the respect shown toward "Indian" religious beliefs and traditions, the sacredness of things, and Wesley's listening to the "Indian" elder in *Star Trek: The Next Generation* "Journey's End."

Although these episodes are fiction, at least the science fiction genre includes "Indians" as part of the universe's collective future, and, when Hollywood writers, directors, and producers are willing, they can portray First Nations peoples, cultures, traditions, and religious beliefs in a positive, respectful, nonstereotypical manner.

Epilogue

I began this discussion on "Indian" stereotypes by explaining the impact that *Star Trek* "The Paradise Syndrome" had on me as a child. The episode carried an apt name. Like J. W. Schultz, an easterner who left New England to take up the ways of the Blackfoot and then published *My Life as an Indian* in 1907, Captain Kirk donned feathers and lived the dominant society's fantasy of "going Native," complete with "noble Indian" leader, the virtuous "Indian princess" to woo and win, and an "evil medicine man" to vanquish.[2] These formulaic characters have recurred in European and Euro-American newspapers and literature, then in the cinema, and, finally, on television. But the daily reality that all First Nations peoples face—being compared with and expected to conform to the stereotypes—is a far cry from the paradise of Kirk's idealistic fantasy or its later incarnations in films and television, including other episodes in the *Star Trek* universe.

Since the *Star Trek: Voyager* series ended in 2001 (although it can now be seen nightly in syndication), the portrayal of First Nations peoples in TV science fiction, as well as in other types of shows, has shrunk to near invisibility once again. For all Chakotay's flaws as an "Indian" in outer space, and Beltran's apathy toward the character he played, Chakotay did provide hope for First Nations youths for the future of Natives—Native who could retain their unique sovereign identity, traditions, and beliefs while, at the same time, working alongside other individuals from diverse cultures.

"Indian" episodes in the early 2000s science fiction shows such as *The X Files* and *The Invisible Man* have backtracked, placing First Nations peoples once more in the category of the "mystic and mysterious" "Indian" stereotype. They are depicted as the "children of nature" who "commune" with Mother Earth, who know and understand her secrets, and as the "good Indian" who assists, shelters, and/or tries to protect the non-Native characters in the episodes, sometimes at the cost of the First Nations individual's life. Here again is another of the five-hundred-year-old stereotypes. The failure of Hollywood writers, directors, and producers to progress beyond these ancient stereotypes and the downward spiral after the pinnacles reached by *Quantum Leap* "Freedom" and *Star Trek: The Next Generation* "Journey's End" are disappointing, to say the least. I hope that these First Nations voices will be heard and listened to and will impact the future of the "Indian" in TV science fiction, as well as in other genres.

Stereotypes do harm. As Carol Cornelius pointed out, students learn about the First Nations peoples through the media, but she also noted that accurate information available to the public and taught in schools "can erase stereotypes."[3] Including First Nations individuals in the Hollywood process and incorporating First Nations voices in how the Indigenous peoples of North America are portrayed in movies and on television would be a good start in erasing stereotypes that have been around for more than five hundred years.

Survey 1 Form

Stereotyping Indigenous Peoples in Science Fiction TV Shows

The information you supply will be identified by a participant number and gender, not by your name and tribal affiliation unless you specify that it is all right to use one or both of these. This information will not be reproduced in its entirety. Please answer the set of questions for each of the four episodes on the tape—*My Favorite Martian* "Go West, Young Martian, Go West" Part II, which aired in 1965; *Star Trek* "The Paradise Syndrome," which aired in 1968; *Quantum Leap* "Freedom," which aired in 1990; and *Star Trek: Voyager* "Tattoo," which aired in 1995. Feel free to add additional comments or observations.

1. What did you like and/or dislike about this episode's depiction of "Indians"?

2. What types of stereotypes did you see in this episode? Why do you think the episode's writer(s) chose these particular stereotypes?

3. In what ways did/didn't the episode reinforce the dominant society's idea of "Indians"?

4. Which stereotypical image affected you (positively or negatively) the most? Why?

5. If you were writing the script for one of these shows, what would you do differently?

Shoshone Survey Form

Stereotyping Indigenous Peoples in Science Fiction TV Shows

The information you supply will be identified by a participant number and gender, not by your name and tribal affiliation unless you specify that it is all right to use one or both of these. This information will not be reproduced in its entirety.

After viewing the video *Quantum Leap* "Freedom," which aired in 1990, please answer the following questions. Feel free to add additional comments or observations.

11. What did you like and/or dislike about this episode's depiction of "Indians"?

12. What types of stereotypes did you see in this episode? Why do you think the episode's writer(s) chose these particular stereotypes?

13. In what ways did/didn't the episode reinforce the dominant society's idea of "Indians"?

14. Which stereotypical image affected you (positively or negatively) the most? Why?

15. If you were writing the script for one of these shows, what would you do differently?

16. Do you think there is anything significant about Sam leaping into a Shoshone man's life in the year 1970? If so, what?

Survey 2 Form

"American Indian" Religions and Spirituality
Stereotyping in Science Fiction TV Shows

The information you supply will be identified by a participant number and gender, not by your name and tribal affiliation unless you specify that it is all right to use one or both of these. This information will not be reproduced in its entirety.

After viewing the video clips, please answer the set of questions for each of the three episodes viewed—*The Adventures of Superman* "Test of a Warrior," which aired in 1954; *Star Trek: The Next Generation* "Journey's End," which aired in 1994; and *Star Trek: Voyager* "The Cloud," which aired in 1995. Feel free to add additional comments or observations.

1. What did you like and/or dislike about this episode's depiction of "Indian spirituality"?

2. What types of stereotypes did you see in this episode? Why do you think the episode's writer(s) chose these particular stereotypes?

3. In what ways did/didn't the episode reinforce the dominant society's idea of "Indian spirituality"?

4. Which stereotypical image affected you (positively or negatively) the most? Why?

5. If you were writing the script for one of these shows, what would you do differently?

Interview Questions for Focus Group

1. Which Indian stereotype(s) bothers you the most? Why?

2. Why do you think Indigenous stereotypes, some dating back as far as five hundred years ago, continue to be used by the dominant society (and found acceptable) today in the modern media?

Categorizing the Comments

Distribution of Positive and Negative Comments on the Episodes, in Order of Airdates

Episode	Number of comments			Number of comment categories	
	Positive	Negative	Total	Positive	Negative
The Adventures of Superman "Test of a Warrior" (1954)	4	136	140	1	15
My Favorite Martian "Go West, Young Martian, Go West, Part II" (1965)	8	109	117	3	18
Star Trek "The Paradise Syndrome" (1968)	1	81	82	1	11
Quantum Leap "Freedom" 1990 (Survey Group 1)	48	38	86	8	9
Quantum Leap "Freedom" 1990 (Shoshone Survey Group)	7	44	51	4	14
Star Trek: The Next Generation "Journey's End" (1994)	49	29	78	6	6
Star Trek: Voyager "The Cloud" (1995)	5	58	63	3	6
Star Trek: Voyager "Tattoo" (1995)	19	44	63	5	16

Major Comment Categories

Comment category	AS	MFM	ST	QL	QLS	STNG	STVC	STVT	Total
Positive									
Positive depiction of "Indian" elders, traditions, culture, religious beliefs, "Indian" people		3		43	6	43	3	16	114
Cast Natives to play Natives		4		4	1	6			15
Miscellaneous comments	4	1	1	1			2	3	12
Negative									
Negative depiction of "Indian" elders, traditions, culture, religious beliefs, "Indian" people, tribe	114	101	72	38	42	29	23	35	454
Offended by way sacred objects used, depicted	16	6	4				25		51
No Natives cast to play Natives	6		5				10	8	29
Miscellaneous comments		2			2			1	5

Note: AS = The Adventures of Superman "Test of a Warrior"; MFM = My Favorite Martian "Go West, Young Martian, Go West, Part II"; ST = Star Trek "The Paradise Syndrome"; QL = Quantum Leap "Freedom" (Survey Group I); QLS = Quantum Leap "Freedom" (Shoshone Survey Group); STNG = Star Trek: The Next Generation "Journey's End"; STVC = Star Trek: Voyager "The Cloud"; STVT = Star Trek: Voyager "Tattoo." For complete comment categories with a breakdown of positive and negative comments per episode, see appendix F.

Common Threads

*Positive and Negative Comments on Stereotypical
Depictions of "Indians" in the Episodes*

The comments of survey participants listed here have been grouped
into broad-based categories.

The Adventures of Superman "Test of a Warrior" (1954)

Positive comments	Negative comments
1. Somewhat amusing in its so overwhelming stereotypical/comic portrayal of "Indians." [4]	1. Lack of respect for elders, traditions, and religious beliefs. [25] 2. Offended by the way sacred objects used/depicted. [16] 3. "Indians" perceived as inferior. [13] 4. "Indians" frozen in the past while whites progress. [13] 5. Whites superior/white religion superior to "Indians." [12] 6. Whites perceiving "Indian" religious beliefs to be foolish. [12] 7. "Indians" not realistic/hokey. [11] 8. "Homogenized Indian" tribe. [10] 9. White savior. [6] 10. No Natives actors. [6] 11. To progress, "Indians" must give up their "Indianness." [3] 12. All leaders are male. [3] 13. "Indians" duped by whites/Superman. [3] 14. "Indians" have abusive culture. [2] 15. "Indians" abuse tobacco. [1]

My Favorite Martian "Go West, Young Martian, Go West, Part II" (1965)

Positive comments	Negative comments
1. Cast Natives to play Natives. [4] 2. Episode kind of OK. [3] 3. Lodges all facing same direction. [1]	1. Lack of respect for elders, traditions, and religious beliefs. [17] 2. "Indians" capture, kill, sacrifice whites. [13] 3. "Indians" perceived as inferior. [10] 4. Inaccurate history/clothing/customs. [10] 5. "Indians" used stilted language. [9] 6. "Indians" easily tricked/duped by whites. [8] 7. Offended by the way sacred objects used/depicted. [6]

(*Continued on page 112*)

My Favorite Martian "Go West, Young Martian, Go West, Part II" (1965) (Continued)

Positive comments	Negative comments
	8. Whites perceiving "Indian" religious beliefs to be foolish. [5]
	9. "Indians" not realistic. [5]
	10. "Indians" frozen in the past while whites progress. [4]
	11. Clichéd "Indians" vs. Cavalry. [4]
	12. Alien/white impersonating a god. [4]
	13. "Indians" barbaric/mean to whites. [4]
	14. "Homogenized Indian" tribe. [3]
	15. Hollywood doesn't care to get it right. [3]
	16. "Indians" made fun of. [2]
	17. "Indians" shown as having no place in modern world. [1]
	18. "Indians" only seen as entertainment. [1]

Star Trek "The Paradise Syndrome" (1968)

Positive comments	Negative comments
1. Liked that Captain Kirk saved the "Indian" boy. [1]	1. "Indians" frozen in the past/don't evolve while whites progress. [15]
	2. "Indians" shown as primitive and will believe anything. [14]
	3. White savior. [11]
	4. "Indians" worship a white man as a god. [9]
	5. "Homogenized Indian" tribe, wearing inappropriate clothing. [7]
	6. Only three tribes considered peaceful enough to deserve saving. [6]
	7. No Native actors. [5]
	8. Lack of respect for elders, traditions, and religious beliefs. [4]
	9. Misuse of traditional Native medicine. [4]
	10. "Indians" uneducated. [3]
	11. "Indians" inferior to whites. [3]

Quantum Leap "Freedom" (1990), Survey Group 1

Positive comments	Negative comments
1. Wise Grandfather who behaves like a real "Indian" grandfather. [13]	1. Sheriff/whites control of "Indians." [12]
2. Grandson realizes the importance of elders/ traditions/culture. [10]	2. "Indians" depicted as thieves and criminals/ commit crimes and escape to the rez. [11]
3. "Indian" humor. [9]	3. "Indians" inferior. [3]
4. Debunking "Indian" mystic powers. [4]	4. Die as a warrior no matter what. [3]
5. Cast Natives to play Natives. [4]	5. Clichéd cowboy-and-Indian chase/ shoot-out. [2]
6. "Indians" dressed in modern clothes. [4]	6. The grandson depicted as having no future or Native interest. [2]
7. Sam and Al impressed with "Indian" culture. [3]	7. "Indians" must assimilate into white culture. [2]
8. The younger generation of "Indians" turn away from the old ways. [1]	8. The only good "Indian" is a dead one. [2]
	9. "Indians" frozen in the past/don't evolve while whites progress. [1]

Quantum Leap "Freedom" (1990), Shoshone Survey Group

Positive comments	Negative comments

1. Elder wanted to die like warrior. [2]
2. Discussed/showed Native issues. [2]
3. "Indian" humor. [2]
4. Cast Natives to play Natives. [1]
	1. Inaccurate setting/culture/customs/
	   traditions. [8]
	2. Lack of respect for elders, traditions, and
	   religious beliefs. [6]
	3. "Indians" depicted as thieves and criminals/
	   commit crimes and escape to the rez. [5]
	4. Don't know Shoshones/don't want to learn. [5]
	5. Stupid humor. [4]
	6. Shoshones don't put elders in nursing
	   home. [3]
	7. Homogenized "Indian" ceremonies. [3]
	8. Don't forget old way/learning traditions. [2]
	9. Whites play "Indians"/"Indians" play whites. [2]
	10. Object to mascots/scalping scenes. [2]
	11. "Indians" frozen in the past/don't evolve while
	   whites progress. [1]
	12. "Mystical" people. [1]
	13. All "Indians" traditional/want to live on rez. [1]
	14. Shoshones live off the government. [1]

Significance to the year 1970. [2]	No significance to the year 1970. [3]

Star Trek: The Next Generation "Journey's End" (1994)

Positive comments	Negative comments

1. Made everything sacred. [15]
2. Respect for "Indian" religious beliefs/
   traditions/elders. [13]
3. Included real history. [8]
4. Cast Natives to play Natives. [6]
5. Showed that history can repeat itself. [4]
6. Depicted non-Plains culture for a change. [3]
	1. Made everything sacred/following traditional
	   religious beliefs. [7]
	2. White guy has superior knowledge and ability
	   about "Indian" religion/chosen. [6]
	3. Stoic personae of "Indians"/stilted
	   language. [6]
	4. The "Indian" turns into an alien. [4]
	5. Picard white savior/advocate. [4]
	6. Inaccurately mixing history/mixing history
	   with fiction. [2]

Star Trek: Voyager "The Cloud" (1995)

Positive comments	Negative comments

1. "Indian" dressed modern so not so much
   the "other." [3]
2. Liked that spirit guide was a lizard, not a
   bear/eagle. [1]
3. Some humor. [1]
	1. Offended by the way sacred objects used/
	   depicted. [25]
	2. Non-Native cast as the "Indian." [10]
	3. Native spirituality romanticized. [7]
	4. Whole episode surreal/hokey/New Age BS. [7]
	5. Mysterious "Indian"/Janeway transfixed by
	   "Indian" religious practices. [6]
	6. Stoic "Indian"/slow speech/sermonizing. [3]

Star Trek: Voyager "Tattoo" (1995)

Positive comments	Negative comments
1. Put "Indians" in outer space. [9]	1. Lack of respect for elders, traditions, and religious beliefs. [11]
2. Generations can differ on cultural teachings. [3]	2. No Natives cast to play Natives. [8]
3. Shows the struggle to keep cultures alive. [3]	3. "Indians" shown as "children of the forest" who are simple/primitive/scared/shy. [4]
4. Shows positive impact of oral history. [2]	4. "Indians" shown as too primitive to have language and culture until white aliens give them to the "Indians." [3]
5. "Indians" shown in the "New World" 45,000 years ago and before whites. [2]	5. "Indian" denial of self and culture. [2]
	6. The drive to maintain cultures not shown. [2]
	7. "Indians" commune with nature. [2]
	8. "Indians" are inferior and Whites rulers. [2]
	9. "Indians" are ignorant and need guidance. [2]
	10. "Indians" are uneducated. [2]
	11. It took aliens to revive "Indian" culture. [1]
	12. White values replace/destroy "Indian" culture. [1]
	13. "Indians" "discovered." [1]
	14. White woman calls the shots. [1]
	15. Put "Indians" in outer space. [1]
	16. "Homogenized Indian" tribe. [1]

Notes

Discussion of Terms Used

1. R. D. Ranade, *Mysticism in India: The Poet-Saints of Maharashtra* (Albany: State University of New York Press, 1983), iii, v.

2. Ibid., v.

3. Ibid., xiii.

4. Tasiwoopa ápi, interview with the author, 1 June 2003.

5. Alice B. Kehoe, "Primal Gaia: Primitivists and Plastic Medicine Men," in *The Invented Indian: Cultural Fictions and Government Policies*, ed. James A. Clifton (New Brunswick, NJ: Transaction Publishers, 1990), 195.

6. Ibid., 193–194.

7. Ibid., 194.

8. Ranade, *Mysticism in India*, 1.

9. Christian F. Feest, "Pride and Prejudice: The Pocahontas Myth and the Pamunkey," in *The Invented Indian: Cultural Fictions and Government Policies*, ed. James A. Clifton (New Brunswick, NJ: Transaction Publishers, 1990), 50.

10. Devon A. Mihesuah, *American Indians: Stereotypes and Realities* (Atlanta: Clarity Press, 1996), 68.

Introduction

1. Unless otherwise noted in citations, all television shows and movies mentioned in this book were taped from television by the author over a period of several years. Air dates, television channels, and production information are cited when available. "The Paradise Syndrome" first aired on NBC on 4 October 1968.

2. Jacquelyn Kilpatrick, *Celluloid Indians: Native Americans and Film* (Lincoln, NE: Bison Books, 1999), xv; Ralph E. Friar and Natasha A. Friar, *The Only Good Indian . . . The Hollywood Gospel* (New York: Drama Book Specialists, 1972), 5–7.

3. Friar and Friar, *The Only Good Indian*, 86.

4. Rennard Strickland, *Tonto's Revenge: Reflections on American Indian Culture and Policy* (Albuquerque: University of New Mexico Press, 1997), 19, 25, 40; Kilpatrick, *Celluloid Indians*, 51.

5. Kilpatrick, *Celluloid Indians*, 51.

6. Andrew J. Orkin, "One Editorial Cartoon, Two Very Different Perceptions," *Toronto Star*, 30 March 2002, A8.

7. Quoted in Francis Paul Prucha, *The Great Father: The United States Government and the American Indians*, abr. ed. (Lincoln: University of Nebraska Press, 1984), 53.

8. John M. Coward, *The Newspaper Indian: Native American Identity in the Press, 1820–90* (Champaign: University of Illinois Press, 1999), 36–37. For a detailed evolution of U.S. "Indian" policy, see Prucha's *Great Father* and *Documents of United States Indian Policy*, 3rd ed. (Lincoln: University of Nebraska Press, 2000).

9. Quoted in Coward, *The Newspaper Indian*, 3.

10. Ibid., 2, 3, 4.

11. Quoted in Allan J. Ryan, *The Trickster Shift: Humour and Irony in Contemporary Native Art* (Seattle: University of Washington Press, 1999),

159. Mohawk artist Bill Powless created a turnabout work of art in pastel in 1978 entitled *Strange Rituals*. In it, a traditionally dressed Mohawk man stands among white disco dancers, taking photos just like whites do to us at pow wows. It's a classic.

12. Linda P. Rouse and Jeffery R. Hanson, "American Indian Stereotyping, Resource Competition, and Status-Based Prejudice," *American Indian Culture and Research Journal* 15.3 (1991): 1–17.

13. Kilpatrick, *Celluloid Indians*, 5.

14. Rouse and Hanson, "American Indian Stereotyping"; Klaus Lubber, *Born for the Shade: Stereotypes of the Native American in United States Literature and the Visual Arts, 1779–1894* (Atlanta: Rodopi, 1994), 14–18.

15. Strickland, *Tonto's Revenge*, 24–25.

16. Ward Churchill, *Fantasies of the Master Race: Literature, Cinema, and the Colonization of American Indians* (Monroe, ME: Common Courage Press, 1992), 167.

17. Linda Tuhiwai Smith, *Decolonizing Methodologies: Research and Indigenous Peoples* (New York: Zed Books, 1999), 1.

18. Ibid., p. 56.

19. Churchill, *Fantasies of the Master Race*, 239.

20. Lubber, *Born for the Shade*, 14–18; Kilpatrick, *Celluloid Indians*, 1–15.

21. Churchill, *Fantasies of the Master Race*, 231, 232; Kilpatrick, *Celluloid Indians*, 12–13; Tim Brooks and Earle Marsh, *The Complete Directory to Prime Time Network and Cable TV Shows 1946–Present*, 7th ed. (New York: Ballantine Books, 1999), xiv, xv.

Chapter 1

1. Myrdene Anderson et al., "A Semiotic Perspective on the Sciences: Steps toward a New Paradigm," *Semiotica* 52 (1984): 7–47.

2. C. T. Coll-Garcia, E. C. Meyers, and L. Brillon, "Ethnic and Minority Parenting," in *Handbook of Parenting*, vol. 2, ed. March Bornstein (Mahwah, NJ: Lawrence Erlbaum, 1995), 189–209; C. R. Cooper and J. Denner, "Theories Linking Culture and Psychology," *Annual Review of Psychology* 49 (1998), 559–584; R. W. Taylor, "The Effects of Economic and Social Stressors on Parenting and Adolescent Adjustment in African-American Families," in *Social and Emotional Adjustment and Family Relations in Ethnic Minority Families*, ed. R. W. Taylor and M. C. Wang (Mahwah, NJ: Lawrence Erlbaum, 1997), 35–52; L. C. Wilson and D. R. William, "Issues in the Quality of Data on Minority Groups," in *Studying Minority Adolescents: Conceptual, Methodological, and Theoretical Issues*, ed. Vonnie McLoyd and Laurence Steinberg (Mahwah, NJ: Lawrence Erlbaum, 1998), 237–250.

3. I. E. Sigel, A. V. McGillicuddy-DeLisi, and J. J. Goodnow, eds., *Parental Belief Systems: The Psychological Consequences for Children*, 2nd ed. (Hillsdale, NJ: Lawrence Erlbaum, 1992), 143–172.

4. Smith, *Decolonizing Methodologies*, 1.

5. Ibid., 2.

Chapter 2

1. Drew Hayden Taylor, *Funny, You Don't Look Like One: Observations from a Blue-Eyed Ojibway* (Penticton, British Columbia: Theytus Books, 1998), 3.

2. Carol Cornelius, *Iroquois Corn in a Culture-Based Curriculum: A Framework for Respectfully Teaching about Cultures* (Albany: State University of New York Press, 1999), xi.

3. Coward, *Newspaper Indian*, 26–27; Robert F. Berkhofer, Jr., "White Conceptions of Indians," in *Handbook of North American Indians*, vol. 4, *History of Indian-White Relations*, ed. Wilcomb E. Washburn (Washington, DC: Smithsonian Institution, 1988), 522.

4. Quoted in Cornelius, *Iroquois Corn*, 2.

5. Quoted in Tim Shaughnessy, "White, Stereotypes of Indians," *Journal of American Indian Education* 17.2 (1978): 1.

6. Ibid.

7. Joseph Marshall III, *On Behalf of the Wolf and the First Peoples* (Santa Fe, NM: Red Crane Books, 1995), 101; Cornel D. Pewewardy, "Fluff and Feathers: Treatment of American Indians in the Literature and the Classroom," *Equity and Excellence in Education* 31.1 (1998): 69.

8. Cornel D. Pewewardy, "Renaming Ourselves on Our Own Terms: Race, Tribal Nations, and Representation in Education," *Indigenous Nations Studies Journal* 1.1 (2000): 17.

9. Cornel D. Pewewardy, "Educators and Mascots: Challenging Contradictions," in *Team Spirits: The Native American Mascots Controversy*, ed. C. Richard King and Charles F. Springwood (Lincoln: University of Nebraska Press, 2001), 257.

10. Ibid., 257–258.

11. Peter Berger and Thomas Luckmann, *The Social Construction of Reality* (London: Allen Lane, 1967), 127.

12. John Clark Ridpath, *History of the World: Being an Account of the Principal Events in the Career of the Human Race from the Beginnings of Civilization to the Present Time Comprising the Development of Social Institutions and the Story of All Nations from Recent and Authentic Sources* (Chicago: Riverside, 1901), vol. 7, 40.

13. Coward, *Newspaper Indian*, 26–27.

14. Ibid.

15. From a lecture by Linda Adler, "Euro and African American Images of American Indians," at Kroch Library on the Cornell University campus, Ithaca, NY, 19 April 2000; Coward, *Newspaper Indian*, 26–27; Berkhofer, "White Conceptions of Indians," 523–524.

16. "Historical Chronicle: Boston," *The American Magazine*, August 1745, 370.

17. Beverly Slapin and Doris Seale, "The Bloody Trail of Columbus Day," in *Through Indian Eyes: The Native Experience in Books for Children*, ed. Beverly Slapin and Doris Seale (Los Angeles: University of California, 1998), 5–6; Doris Seale, "Let Us Put Our Minds Together and See What Life We Will Make for Our Children," in Slapin and Seale, *Through Indian Eyes*, 10, 11; James Wilson, *The Earth Shall Weep: A History of Native America* (New York: Grove Press, 1998), 94–96.

18. Quoted in Grant Foreman, *Indian Removal* (1932; repr., Norman: University of Oklahoma Press, 1972), 351.

19. Quoted in Beverly Slapin, introduction to Slapin and Seale, *Through Indian Eyes*, 2.

20. Coward, *Newspaper Indian*, 5–6.

21. "The Recent Events," *The Southern Banner*, 23 March 1833.

22. Prucha, *Great Father*, 75–77.

23. Kilpatrick, *Celluloid Indians*, 48.

24. Mihesuah, *American Indians*, 20; Kilpatrick, *Celluloid Indians*, 9.

25. Lyman Horace Weeks and Edwin M. Bacon, *An Historical Digest of the Provincial Press 1689–1783* (Boston: Society for Americana), i.

26. Wilson, *The Earth Shall Weep*, 96; Adler lecture.

27. Adler lecture; Wilson, *The Earth Shall Weep*, 126.

28. Barbara Perkins, Robyn Warhol, and George Perkins, *Woman's Work: An Anthology of American Literature* (New York: McGraw-Hill), 46.

29. Robert W. Venables, *Crowded Wilderness: American Indians, the United States, and the Five Hundred Year War for Indian America* (Ithaca, NY: Cornell University, 1999), 67.

30. Mason Wade, "French Indian Policies," in Washburn, *Handbook of North American Indians*, vol. 4, *History of Indian-White Relations*, 20; Wilbur R. Jacobs, "British Indian Policies to 1783," in Washburn, *Handbook of North American Indians*,

vol. 4, *History of Indian-White Relations*, 5.

31. "History of the Treatment of Prisoners among the American Indians," *The American Museum, or Repository*, May 1789, 469.

32. Wilson, *The Earth Shall Weep*, 123; Seale, "Let Us Put Our Minds Together," 10; Cornelius, *Iroquois Corn*, 3.

33. Among various texts, her real name has been spelled as Matoaka, Matowaka, Matoka, Matoaks, and Matoax. Frances Mossiker, *Pocahontas: The Life and the Legend* (New York: Da Capo Press, 1996), 41.

34. The name "Pocahontas" has also been spelled as Pochantes and Pokahantesu, and it means something to the effect of "playful, sportive, frolicsome, mischievous, frisky." Quoted in Mossiker, *Pocahontas*, 41. Her father supposedly gave the nickname to her.

35. Variations on this stereotype include the ever-faithful sidekick of movie and TV fame, Tonto, and any "Indian" who turns his or her back on "Indian" culture to follow "civilized" ways, as Pocahontas did in this 1755 "pseudo-history." Coward, *Newspaper Indian*, 7; Kilpatrick, *Celluloid Indians*, 1–15, 151–153; Strickland, *Tonto's Revenge*, 18–25.

36. Mossiker, *Pocahontas*, 91–92.

37. "An Account of the First Confederacy of the Six Nations, and Their Present Tributaries, Dependents, and Allies, and of Their Religion, and Form of Government," *The American Magazine*, December 1744, 669.

38. Ibid.

39. Reginald Horsman, *Race and Manifest Destiny: The Origins of American Racial Anglo-Saxonism* (Cambridge, MA: Harvard University Press, 1981), 189–190.

40. "Advices from America," *The British Magazine, or Monthly Repository for Gentlemen and Ladies*, August 1760, 500.

41. Douglas Edward Leach, "Colonial Indian Wars," in Washburn, *Handbook of North American Indians*, vol. 4, *History of Indian-White Relations*, 137.

42. Adler lecture; Coward, *Newspaper Indian*, 28–29.

43. "Advices from America," 500–501.

44. R. S. Cotterill, *The Southern Indians: The Story of the Civilized Tribes before Removal* (Norman: University of Oklahoma Press, 1954), 28–29; J. Leitch Wright, Jr., *The Only Land They Knew: American Indians in the Old South* (Lincoln: University of Nebraska Press, 1999), 145.

45. Adler lecture; "Dialogue between Mercury—An English Duelists—A North-American Savage," in *The British Magazine, or Monthly Repository for Gentlemen and Ladies*, March 1760, 118–119.

46. "Dialogue between Mercury," 119.

47. Ibid.

48. Ibid., 120.

49. I had a Mohawk student who told me that when she was in elementary school, she had gone home in tears one day after an American history class. The teacher had taught, as part of the American Revolution, that the Mohawks had practiced treachery and cannibalism for centuries until they were "conquered" during the revolution. The student said she had asked her mother if her ancestors were really cannibals. Her mother, furious with the teacher for repeating the misconceptions about Mohawks that have been perpetuated since colonial times, gave her daughter her first lesson in inaccurate stereotypes and the dominant society's ready acceptance of them as the truth with a capital "T."

50. "Advices from America," 500; "American News," *The British Magazine, or Monthly Repository for Gentlemen and Ladies*, September 1760, 559.

51. Cotterill, *The Southern Indians*,

28–29; Wright, *The Only Land They Knew*, 145.

52. Ibid.

53. "Advices from America," 500; "American News," 559.

54. John M. Coward, interview with the author, 1 September 2000.

55. "Manner in which the American Indians carry on war—causes of war among them—encroachments on their hunting grounds,—emulation—ardour of the young warriors—spirit of revenge—their war councils and embassices," *The American Museum, or Repository*, February 1789, 147.

56. James Axtell, *The European and the Indian: Essays in the Ethnohistory of Colonial North America* (New York: Oxford University Press, 1981), 208–210, 312; Wilson, *The Earth Shall Weep*, 97; Foreman, *Indian Removal*, 351; lecture by Daniel Usner, "American Indian History 1500–1850," Cornell University, Ithaca, NY, 10 February 1999.

57. In his book, Takaki, the grandson of Japanese immigrants to Hawaii, contests the "American melting pot" myth and compels readers to view American society through a multitude of ethnic voices rather than through the singleness of the dominant society's words. Ronald Takaki, *A Different Mirror: A History of Multicultural America* (New York: Little, Brown, 1993).

58. Benjamin Franklin, "Remarks on the North American Indians," in *The American Museum, or Repository*, April 1789, 344.

59. Peter Gay, *The Enlightenment: An Interpretation*, vol. 1, *The Rise of Modern Paganism* (New York: W. W. Norton, 1966), 338–340, 343, 347; Ernst Cassirer, *The Philosophy of the Enlightenment*, trans. Fritz C. A. Koelln and James P. Pettegrove (Princeton, NJ: Princeton University Press, 1951), 175.

60. Cassirer, *The Philosophy of the Enlightenment*, 171.

61. Franklin, "Remarks on the North American Indians," 346.

62. Francis Dana, Edward Wigglesforth, and Peter Thacher, "Petition of the Society for Propagating the Gospel among the Indians and Others in North America, to the Honourable the Senate, and the Honourable House of Representatives, of the Commonwealth of Massachusetts," *The American Museum, or Repository*, November 1789, 430–431.

63. Coward, *Newspaper Indian*, 6.

64. Ibid., 7.

65. Marshall, *On Behalf of the Wolf*, 111.

66. Quoted in S. Elizabeth Bird, "Not My Fantasy: The Persistence of Indian Imagery in *Dr. Quinn: Medicine Woman*," in *Dressing in Feathers: The Construction of the Indian in American Popular Culture*, ed. S. Elizabeth Bird (New York: Westview Press, 1996), 249–250.

67. Strickland, *Tonto's Revenge*, 23; Annette M. Taylor, "Cultural Heritage in *Northern Exposure*," in Bird, *Dressing in Feathers*, 236; Marshall, *On Behalf of the Wolf*, 28, 111; Kilpatrick, *Celluloid Indians*, 151–153.

68. Kilpatrick, *Celluloid Indians*, 15; Coward, *Newspaper Indian*, 7.

69. Coward, *Newspaper Indian*, 4–6; Kilpatrick, *Celluloid Indians*, 2.

70. Kilpatrick, *Celluloid Indians*, 3.

71. Mihesuah, *American Indians*, 29, 37, 48, 54, 76; Strickland, *Tonto's Revenge*, 18, 41; Kilpatrick, *Celluloid Indians*, 2, 8, 47.

72. Friar and Friar, *The Only Good Indian*, (New York: Drama Book Specialists, 1972), 56; Kilpatrick, *Celluloid Indians*, 49; Strickland, *Tonto's Revenge*, 24–25.

73. Kilpatrick, *Celluloid Indians*, 15.

74. Churchill, *Fantasies of the Master Race*, 233.

75. Taylor, "Cultural Heritage in *Northern Exposure*," 233.

76. Andrew Macdonald, Gina Macdonald, and Mary Ann Sheridan, *Shape-shifting: Images of Native*

Americans in Recent Popular Fiction (Westport, CT: Greenwood Press, 2000), 243–256.

77. Ibid., 245.

78. "Test of a Warrior" originally aired in 1954. Quote from Brooks and Marsh, *Complete Directory*, 18.

79. Brooks and Marsh, *Complete Directory*, 835.

80. "Freedom" originally aired on NBC on 14 February 1990.

81. "Journey's End" originally aired in 1994.

82. Jerry Mander, *In the Absence of the Sacred: The Failure of Technology and the Survival of the Indian Nations* (San Francisco: Sierra Book Club, 1991), 97.

Chapter 3

1. Shari M. Huhndorf, *Going Native: Indians in the American Cultural Imagination* (Ithaca, NY: Cornell University Press, 2001), 27.

2. Robert Rydell, *All the World's a Fair: Visions of Empire at American International Expositions, 1876–1916* (Chicago: University of Chicago Press, 1984), 25.

3. Tasiwoopa ápi, interview with the author, 1 June 2003.

4. Kilpatrick, *Celluloid Indians*, 9.

5. Originally this episode was presented in two parts. "Part I" did not feature First Nations individuals in the plot; it originally aired on CBS on 12 September 1965. "Part II" originally aired on CBS a week later, on 19 September.

6. Tim O'Hara (played by Bill Bixby), a newspaper reporter for the *Los Angeles Sun*, finds a Martian and his one-man spaceship. Thinking he will have the scoop of the century, Tim brings the Martian to his over-the-garage apartment while the Martian repairs his spacecraft, which is hidden in the garage. As an explanation for the Martian's presence, Tim tells his landlady, Mrs. Brown (played by Pamela Britton), that the Martian is his uncle Martin. Played by Alan Hewitt, Detective Brennan is Mrs. Brown's boyfriend. He is suspicious of Tim and "Uncle Martin"; therefore Brennan constantly snoops around.

7. Mihesuah, *American Indians*, 12.

8. "Historic California Posts: Fort Yuma," California State Military Museum, California State Military Department, http://www.military museum.org/FtYuma.html.

9. Ibid.

10. Ibid.

11. Strickland, *Tonto's Revenge*, 21.

12. Arrel Morgan Gibson, *The American Indian: Prehistory to the Present* (Lexington, MA: D. C. Heath, 1980), 30.

13. http://www.itcaonline.com/tribes_quechan.html, http://www.militarymuseum.org/ftyuma.html, http://www.ihs.gov/facilitiesservices/areaofficers/phoenix/phx_su_ftyuma.cfm, and http://www.primenet.com/~itca/tribes/quechan.htm.

14. Tasiwoopa ápi, interview with the author, 7 October 2002.

15. Strickland, *Tonto's Revenge*, 18.

16. Gibson, *The American Indian*, 75, 76.

17. Handbook, 373; Ellsworth Huntington, *The Red Man's Continent* (New Haven, CT: Yale University Press, 1919), 139.

18. Quoted in Kilpatrick, *Celluloid Indians*, 47, 48.

19. Adler lecture.

20. Quoted in Huntington, *Red Man's Continent*, 139.

21. Brooks and Marsh, *Complete Directory*, 699.

22. Hedley Donovan et al., eds., *The Indians* (New York: Time-Life Books, 1973), 124.

23. Tasiwoopa ápi, interview with the author, 7 October 2002.

24. Strickland, *Tonto's Revenge*, 19.

25. Prucha, *Great Father*, 345.

26. Adler lecture.

27. Friar and Friar, *The Only Good*

Indian, 229, 230, 238; Strickland, *Tonto's Revenge,* 19.

28. Friar and Friar, *The Only Good Indian,* 244.

29. Ibid., 229, 233.

30. Kilpatrick, *Celluloid Indians,* 46.

31. Ibid.

32. Quoted in ibid.

33. Duane Champagne, *Native America: Portrait of the Peoples* (Detroit: Visible Ink Press, 1994), 131–132; Venables, *Crowded Wilderness,* 40–42.

34. Kilpatrick, *Celluloid Indians,* 51.

35. Champagne, *Native America,* 131.

36. Kilpatrick, *Celluloid Indians,* 48, 51.

37. Ibid., 9.

38. Quoted in ibid., 34.

39. Kilpatrick, *Celluloid Indians,* 65.

40. The episode originally aired on UPN on 6 November 1995.

41. Rubber trees are actually Amazonian, not Central American.

42. Neelix is a Talaxian, a race indigenous to the Delta Quadrant. He is *Voyager*'s chef, a diplomatic adviser to the captain, and also the morale officer for *Voyager.*

43. Tuvok is a Vulcan and the head of security for *Voyager.*

44. See http://www.startrek.com.

45. The first two seasons of *Star Trek: Voyager* were the only ones to deal with Chakotay's cultural roots to any extent. After that, there were isolated references, but nothing of substance (by the show's standards of substance). The "medicine bundle" and the high-tech device appeared in the *Star Trek: Voyager* episode entitled "The Cloud," which originally aired on 13 February 1995; directed by David Livingston; featuring Kate Mulgrew, Robert Beltran, Angela Dohrmann, and Judy Geeson, KMCI, Lawrence, KS, 28 August 2000.

46. From the *Star Trek: Voyager* episode entitled "Cathexis," which originally aired on 5 January 1995; directed by Kim Friedman; featuring Kate Mulgrew, Robert Beltran, Brian

Markinson, and Michael Cumpsty, KMCI, Lawrence, KS, 6 September 2000. A discussion of the inaccuracies in the First Nations cultural and stereotypical views on Indigenous peoples depicted in the "Cathexis" episode alone would require its own book.

47. See "Robert Beltran ('Chakotay'—VOY)," transcript of online chat, 4 March 1999, http://www.startrek .com/startrek/view/community/ chat/archive/transcript/1210.html.

48. Participant 6, female.

49. Participant 8, male.

50. Participant 7, female, science fiction fan.

51. Participant 10, male.

52. Participant 18, male, science fiction fan.

53. Participant 4, male.

54. Participant 14, male.

55. Participant 3, female.

56. Participant 21, female, science fiction fan.

57. Venables, *Crowded Wilderness,* 35; John Reid, *A Law of Blood: The Primitive Law of the Cherokee Nation* (New York: New York University Press, 1970), 140.

58. Participant 5, female.

59. Participant 7, female, science fiction fan.

60. James E. Seaver, *A Narrative of the Life of Mrs. Mary Jemison* (1824; repr., New York: Random House, 1929), vi–vii, 38.

61. Ibid., 44, 58–59, 64.

62. Ibid., vii; Carol Berkin, *First Generations: Women in Colonial America* (New York: Hill and Wang, 1997), 61–62.

63. Participant 21, female, science fiction fan.

64. Participant 15, male.

65. Participant 14, male.

66. Participant 7, female, science fiction fan.

67. Tasiwoopa ápi, interview with the author, 2004.

68. Participant 10, male.

69. Ibid.

70. Participant 9, female.

71. Participant 2, male.

72. Participant 21, female, science fiction fan.

73. Ibid.

74. Participant 11, female.

75. Participant 4, male.

76. Participant 21, female, science fiction fan.

77. Participant 7, female, science fiction fan.

78. Participant 6, female.

79. Participant 21, female, science fiction fan.

80. Participant 9, female; participant 19, male.

81. Participant 7, female, science fiction fan.

82. Mihesuah, *American Indians*, 15.

83. Participant 12, female.

84. Participant 16, female.

85. Participant 10, male.

86. Participant 2, male.

87. Participant 5, female.

88. Participant 10, male.

89. Ibid.

90. Ibid.

91. Participant 3, female.

92. Participant 19, male.

93. Participant 3, female.

94. Participant 15, male.

95. Participant 21, female, science fiction fan.

96. Participant 10, male.

97. Participant 20, female, science fiction fan.

98. Participant 21, female, science fiction fan. Mihesuah discusses this stereotype extensive in her book *American Indians: Stereotypes and Realities*. She insists: "It is a mistake to generalize Indians, just as it is incorrect to generalize Europeans, Africans, Hispanics, or Asians. . . . Indians as well as their cultures and traditions change over time, in response to the conditions around them. They are not static. New ideas meld with old ones" (16), just as much as they do in other societies. Nevertheless, the "vanishing red man"

theory, popular throughout the 1800s and beyond, has manifested itself in the stereotypical portrayal of "Indians" as frozen in time, not progressing, not becoming civilized, and not evolving into modern (or futuristic) times (74–75), as seen in the episodes discussed in this work.

99. Participant 18, male, science fiction fan.

100. *Star Trek IV: The Voyage Home* came out in 1986.

101. The *Star Trek* episode "Mirror, Mirror" aired on 6 October 1967 in the show's second season. "The Paradise Syndrome" aired during the show's third and final season.

102. Participant 7, female, science fiction fan.

103. Participant 5, female.

104. Participant 11, female.

105. Participant 28, male.

106. Strickland, *Tonto's Revenge*, 39.

107. Participant 14, male.

108. Participant 23, male.

109. Participant 15, male.

110. Participant 7, female, science fiction fan.

111. Participant 9, female.

112. Participant 12, female.

113. Participant 20, female, science fiction fan.

114. Participant 6, female.

115. Participant 19, male.

116. See "traditional" in the section "Discussion of Terms Used."

117. Participant 16, female.

118. Participant 24, female.

119. Quoted in Kilpatrick, *Celluloid Indians*, 47.

120. Participant 8, male.

121. Participant 20, female, science fiction fan.

122. Participant 7, female, science fiction fan.

123. Kilpatrick, *Celluloid Indians*, 33, 34.

124. Participant 13, female.

125. Participant 17, male.

126. Participant 1, female, science fiction fan.

127. Participant 10, male. No information is available about the supporting actors' ethnic background.

128. Participant 17, male.

129. Participant 7, female, science fiction fan.

130. Participant 1, female, science fiction fan.

131. Participant 13, female.

132. Participant 1, female, science fiction fan.

133. Ibid.

134. Participant 13, female.

135. Participant 4, male.

136. Participant 15, male.

137. Participant 6, female.

138. Participant 24, female.

139. Participant 21, female.

140. Participant 22, male.

141. Participant 11, female.

142. Steven Reddicliffe et al., eds., "Star Trek: A Timeless Guide to the Trek Universe," special thirty-fifth anniversary tribute issue, *TV Guide*, July 2002, 21.

143. Ibid.

144. Ibid.

145. Participant 7, female, science fiction fan.

146. Participant 35, female, science fiction fan.

147. Participant 13, female.

148. Participant 10, male.

149. Participant 13, female.

150. Participant 7, female, science fiction fan.

Chapter 4

1. Demitri B. Shimkin, "Eastern Shoshone," in Washburn, *Handbook of North American Indians*, vol. 4, *History of Indian-White Relations*, 310–311.

2. Ibid., 327.

3. Mihesuah, *American Indians*, 11.

4. This episode, "The Wrong Stuff," aired on 6 November 1991, during the show's fourth season.

5. Brooks and Marsh, *Complete Directory*, 835.

6. Chief Oren Lyons and John Mohawk, eds., *Exiled in the Land of the Free: Democracy, Indian Nations, and the U.S. Constitution* (Santa Fe, NM: Clear Light Publishers, 1992), 334; Alvin M. Josephy, Jr., Joane Nagel, and Troy Johnson, eds., *Red Power: The American Indians' Fight for Freedom*, 2nd ed. (Lincoln, NE: Bison Books, 1999), 44–45, 48.

7. Josephy, Nagel, and Johnson, *Red Power*, 49; Peter Matthiessen, *In the Spirit of Crazy Horse* (1980; repr., Viking Penguin, 1991), 171–173, 193. For more information of these events, see Matthiessen's *In the Spirit of Crazy Horse*.

8. Laurie Anne Whitt, "Cultural Imperialism and the Marketing of Native America," *Contemporary Native American Cultural Issues*, ed. Duane Champagne (Walnut Creek, CA: Altamira Press, 1999), 176. For additional information, see Whitt's section on the cultural politics of ownership, pp. 173–177, and my *News from Indian Country* articles "Western Shoshone Chair Found Dead in Homicide Case" (mid-March 2000, 3A) and "Struggle for Control of Council at Winnemucca" and "Wasson and Other Western Shoshone Leaders Fought for Tribal Rights under the 1863 Treaty of Ruby Valley" (mid-April 2000, 9A).

9. Mihesuah, *American Indians*, 48.

10. Participant 21, female, science fiction fan.

11. Participant 5, female.

12. Participant 15, male.

13. Participant 17, male.

14. Participant 13, female.

15. Participant 21, female, science fiction fan.

16. Participant 13, female.

17. Kent Nerburn, *Neither Wolf nor Dog: On Forgotten Roads with an Indian Elder* (Novato, CA: New World Library, 1994), 68.

18. Marshall, *On Behalf of the Wolf*, 28.

19. Participant 20, female, science fiction fan.

20. Participant 1, female, science fiction fan.

21. Marshall, *On Behalf of the Wolf*, 18.

22. Ibid.

23. Participant 1, female, science fiction fan.

24. Participant 21, female, science fiction fan.

25. Participant 16, female.

26. Participant 10, male.

27. Participant 13, female.

28. Participant 7, female, science fiction fan.

29. Participant 1, female, science fiction fan.

30. Participant 7, female, science fiction fan.

31. Participant 17, male.

32. Participant 7, female, science fiction fan.

33. Participant 8, male.

34. Participant 20, female, science fiction fan.

35. Participant 21, female, science fiction fan.

36. The most infamous of the boarding schools was the Carlisle Indian Industrial School, run by army officer Richard Henry Pratt. He conceived and instituted the policy "kill the Indian and save the man" (Marshall, *On Behalf of the Wolf*, 141). At the first pow wow ever held on the Carlisle school grounds as part of the county's 250th anniversary, Kiowa Pulitzer Prize–winning novelist N. Scott Momaday stated that the policy should be "save the Indian and save the man" (Sierra Adare, "Remembering Carlisle Indian School," *News from Indian Country*, 10B). Tommy Porter, a Mohawk who chose to not attend the memorial pow wow because of the way his ancestor had been treated at the school, said, "At Carlisle there was a lot of destruction of the retention of Indian language, spirit, customs—the basic foundation of everything we stand for" (Adare, "Remembering Carlisle Indian School," 10B).

37. Participant 9, female.

38. Participant 1, female, science fiction fan.

39. Ibid.

40. Participant 13, female.

41. Participant 56, female, science fiction fan.

42. Participant 60, female, science fiction fan.

43. Participant 58, female.

44. Participant 64, male, science fiction fan.

45. Participant 65, male.

46. Participant 57, female.

47. Participant 62, female, science fiction fan.

48. Participant 59, female.

49. Participant 62, female, science fiction fan.

50. Participant 59, female.

51. Participant 60, female, science fiction fan.

52. Participant 65, male.

53. Participant 63, male.

54. Participant 65, male.

55. Participant 59, female.

56. Ibid.

57. Participant 63, male.

58. Participant 65, male.

59. Participant 57, female.

60. Participant 61, female.

61. Participant 63, male.

62. Participant 57, female.

63. Participant 56, female, science fiction fan.

64. Nancy Parezo, "American Indian Stereotypes: Persistent Cultural Blindness," in "Native Identities and Stereotypes," ed. Jodi Brushia et al., focus issue, Red Ink 9.2/10.1 (2002), 43.

65. Participant 64, male, science fiction fan.

66. Sierra Adare, *The Wyoming Guide* (Golden, CO: Fulcrum Publishing, 1999), 97, 98.

67. Demitri B. Shimkin, "Eastern Shoshone," in *Handbook of North American Indians*, vol. 11, *Great Basin*, ed. Warren L. d'Azevedo (Washington, DC: Smithsonian Institution, 1986), 324.

68. Participant 64, male, science fiction fan.

69. Ibid.

70. Participant 62, female, science fiction fan.

71. Participant 61, female.

72. Ibid.

73. Cornel D. Pewewardy, "I'm Not Your Indian Mascot Anymore: Countering the Assault of Indian Mascots in Schools," in Jodi Brushia et al., "Native Identities and Stereotypes," 58–62.

74. Mihesuah, *American Indians*, 110.

75. Ibid., 110–111.

76. Participant 62, female, science fiction fan.

77. Participant 56, female, science fiction fan.

78. Quoted in Ryan, *Trickster Shift*, 72.

79. Participant 60, female, science fiction fan.

80. Participant 58, female.

81. Participant 60, female, science fiction fan.

82. Participant 61, female.

83. Adler lecture.

84. Participant 58, female.

85. Beth Brant, "The Good Red Road," in Champagne, *Contemporary Native American Cultural Issues*, 98–99.

86. Participant 56, female, science fiction fan.

87. Participant 65, male.

88. Wilson, *The Earth Shall Weep*, 43–45.

89. Participant 60, female, science fiction fan.

90. Participant 62, female, science fiction fan.

91. Prucha, *Documents of United States Indian Policy*, 289.

92. Prucha, *Great Father*, 280–281.

93. Ibid., 51.

94. Ibid., 53.

95. Quoted in Prucha, *Great Father*, 102.

96. Participant 56, female, science fiction fan.

97. Ibid.

98. Participant 58, female.

99. The 1998 movie *Smoke Signals* was written by Sherman Alexie, directed by Chris Eyre, and coproduced by Alexie, Eyre, Roger Baerwolf, and others at Shadow Catcher Entertainment. It was the first all-Native feature film to be distributed by a major movie studio.

100. Participant 63, male.

101. Participant 65, male.

102. Participant 62, female, science fiction fan.

103. Participant 57, female.

104. Participant 20, female, science fiction fan.

105. Participant 7, female, science fiction fan.

Chapter 5

1. Vine Deloria, Jr., *God Is Red: A Native View of Religion* (1974; repr., Golden, CO: Fulcrum Publishing, 1994), 239.

2. Churchill, *Fantasies of the Master Race*, 220, 223.

3. Scott B. Vickers, *Native American Identities: From Stereotype to Archetype in Art and Literature* (Albuquerque: University of New Mexico Press, 1998), 42.

4. Brooks and March, *Complete Directory*, 18.

5. "Peace pipe" is Hollywood "Indian-speak"; Deloria, *God Is Red*, 40.

6. For two prime examples of more recent shows that illustrate this type of blending, see *Poltergeist: The Legacy* "Shadow Fall," which aired 27 June 1997, and *Millennium* "A Single Blade of Grass," which aired 24 October 1997.

7. Deloria, *God Is Red*, 43.

8. Ibid., 40, 43.

9. The Traveler first appeared in a *Star Trek: The Next Generation* episode entitled "Where No One Has Gone," which originally aired on 26 October 1987.

10. Susan Berry Brill de Ramirez,

Contemporary American Indian Literatures and the Oral Tradition (Tucson: University of Arizona Press, 1999), 96–97; Deloria, *God Is Red*, 271.

11. Deloria, *God Is Red*, 196–197.

12. Ibid., 38.

13. "Kiva" means "ceremonial room" in the Hopi language; "Chaco Canyon," National Park Service, http://www.nps.gov/chcu.

14. The ruins of Casa Rinconada, the "Great Kiva" in Chaco Canyon, represent one of the largest kivas found in the United States and offer only a hint of the grandeur of this very sacred site; ibid.

15. I am not suggesting that the *Star Trek: The Next Generation* episode had anything whatsoever to do with the takeover of the Mesa Verde kiva. Nevertheless, the occurrence of this incident during the same year that the episode aired does exemplify the pervasiveness and the aggressive nature of the New Agers' tendency to usurp First Nations peoples' religions during the 1990s.

16. Deborah Frazier, "New Agers Damaging Artifacts They Value," *Rocky Mountain News*, 23 June 1994, 8A.

17. Vickers, *Native American Identities*, 43.

18. Quoted in Churchill, *Fantasies of the Master Race*, 223–224.

19. Vickers, *Native American Identities*, 4.

20. There's a particular irony here in that the non-Native actor who plays Chakotay, Robert Beltran, also starred in the made-for-TV movie *Mystic Warrior*, based on the novel *Hanta Yo*, by Ruth Beebe Hill, which totally misrepresented Lakota traditions, culture, religion, and life; Deloria, *God Is Red*, 41–42.

21. See http://www.startrek.com/startrek/view/series/VOY/episode/68830.html.

22. Therefore, one might assume that Chakotay belonged to the Puebloan peoples shown in the *Star Trek: The Next Generation* episode "Journey's End" (see chapter 3). This is not the case, but viewers don't learn this until the second season in an episode named "Tattoo," which originally aired on 6 November 1995.

23. These were back-to-back episodes in the fourth season. "Mortal Coil" aired on 17 December 1997 and "Waking Moments" on 14 January 1998.

24. A Lakota trickster/"tricky spider fellow" named Iktomi that might be the basis of the being A-koo-chee-moya that Chakotay calls on during the animal guide ceremony for the captain, although the pronunciation is way off in that case; Ed McGaa, *Native Wisdom: Perceptions of the Natural Way* (Minneapolis: Four Directions Publishing, 1995), 232, 234.

25. Participant 30, female, science fiction fan.

26. It's a sad irony that the New Age preemptors of traditional religions "preferred to learn from non-Indians who posed as experts in the field" of "Indian culture and religion"; Deloria, *God Is Red*, 42.

27. For more information on this, see the discussion in the next portion of this section.

28. Participant 39, female.

29. Participant 37, female, science fiction fan.

30. Participant 47, female, science fiction fan.

31. Participant 39, female.

32. Participant 48, female, science fiction fan.

33. Participant 54, female.

34. Participant 38, male.

35. Participant 39, female.

36. Participant 41, female, science fiction fan.

37. Participant 47, female, science fiction fan.

38. Participant 44, male, science fiction fan.

39. Participant 45, female, science fiction fan.

40. Participant 49, female.

41. Participant 53, female.

42. Participant 37, female, science fiction fan.

43. Participant 42, female, science fiction fan.

44. Participant 54, female.

45. Participant 39, female; participant 45, female, science fiction fan.

46. Participant 43, female.

47. Participant 48, female. science fiction fan.

48. Participant 42, female, science fiction fan.

49. Participant 48, female, science fiction fan.

50. Participant 42, female, science fiction fan.

51. Participant 57, female, science fiction fan.

52. Participant 50, male, science fiction fan.

53. Participant 43, female.

54. Participant 54. female.

55. Participant 51, female, science fiction fan.

56. Participant 47, female, science fiction fan.

57. Participant 38, male.

58. Participant 46, female, science fiction fan.

59. See note 36 in chapter 3.

60. Although many of the participants who volunteered information listed themselves as following only the traditional spiritual beliefs of their tribe, all of those who classified themselves as Judeo-Christian also listed following the traditional spiritual beliefs of their tribe.

61. Participant 50, male, science fiction fan.

62. Participant 39, female.

63. Participant 55, male.

64. Participant 43, female.

65. Participant 47, female, science fiction fan.

66. Ramirez, *Contemporary American Indian Literatures*, 100.

67. Participant 45, female, science fiction fan.

68. Participant 37, female, science fiction fan.

69. Participant 42, female, science fiction fan.

70. Both quotes in this sentence: participant 41, female, science fiction fan.

71. Participant 45, female, science fiction fan.

72. Participant 53, female.

73. Participant 42, female, Sci-fi fan.

74. Participant 44, male, science fiction fan.

75. Participant 46, female, science fiction fan.

76. Participant 45, female, science fiction fan.

77. Participant 49, female.

78. Participant 51, female, science fiction fan.

79. Participant 53, female.

80. Participant 43, female.

81. Participant 37, female, science fiction fan.

82. See "shape shifters" in the section "Discussion of Terms Used."

83. Participant 37, female, science fiction fan.

84. Participant 48, female, science fiction fan.

85. Participant 42, female, science fiction fan.

86. Participant 47, female, science fiction fan.

87. Participant 10, male.

88. Participant 50, male, science fiction fan.

89. Participant 37, female, science fiction fan.

90. Participant 51, female, science fiction fan.

91. Participant 50, male, science fiction fan.

92. Participant 46, female.

93. Participant 42, female, science fiction fan. See chapter 3 for a complete discussion of the Rubber Tree People and Chakotay's "Indian" ancestry in the episode "Tattoo."

94. Participant 51, female, science fiction fan.

95. Ibid.

96. Ibid.

97. Participant 44, male, science fiction fan.

98. Participant 53, female.

99. Participant 41, female, science fiction fan.

100. Participant 32, male, science fiction fan.

Chapter 6

1. Churchill, *Fantasies of the Master Race*, 167; Mihesuah, *American Indians*, 92–94.

2. Deloria, *God Is Red*, 42; Churchill, *Fantasies of the Master Race*, 167.

3. Participant 36, female.

4. The question regarding the significance of the year 1970 was asked only of Shoshones who viewed the Shoshone episode "Freedom" in the *Quantum Leap* series.

5. Participant 24, female.

6. A prime example was a movie newsreel short-subject series called *Unique Occupations*, which was produced three years after this Superman episode. In one short film titled "Navajo Sand Painting" (now in the author's personal collection), the narrator classified the "medicine man" as a "tribal sorcerer" who has "magical powers" and performs "incantations" to "placate their [the tribe's] protecting gods of the western desert."

7. Participant 42, female, science fiction fan.

8. In hopes of encouraging the Washington Redskins to drop its derogatory moniker, seven prominent First Nations peoples filed a case with the Federal Trademark Trial and Appeal Board in 1992. In 1999 the board ruled that the name "Redskins" and the logo used by the National Football League team were disparaging to Natives and voided the Washington Redskins' trademark rights; Richard King and Charles Fruehling Springwood, *Team Spirits: The Native American Mascots Controversy* (Lincoln, NE: Bison Books,

2001), 4. King and Springwood contend that "through fragments thought to be Indian—a headdress, tomahawk, war paint, or buckskin—Native American mascots reduce them to a series of well-worn clichés, sideshow props, and racist stereotypes, masking, if not erasing, the complexities of Native American experiences and identities" (7). For more information on this heated debate, see King and Springwood's *Team Spirits*.

9. The character B'Elanna was half Klingon (her mother) and half Earthling (her father). B'Elanna spent most of the series trying to ignore or disown her Klingon half and generally didn't practice Klingon traditions or customs, which was why her mother was on the Barge of the Dead, carrying B'Elanna's disgrace. In Klingon religious beliefs, the Barge of the Dead takes doomed souls to Gre'thor, the Klingon version of Hell, but a person can save misfortunate loved ones so that their souls go to Sto-Vo-Kor, Klingon heaven. This episode, titled "Barge of the Dead," aired originally on 6 October 1999.

10. The Star Fleet Prime Directive was established in the original *Star Trek* series and continued throughout the four series. It was a mandate that no one in Star Fleet would tamper with, manipulate, alter, or in any way interfere with any group, race, or planet's culture or development. Captain Kirk ignored this on several occasions throughout the original series.

11. Rick Berman was the executive producer and cocreator of the *Star Trek: Voyager* series.

12. Participant 7, female, science fiction fan.

13. Participant 30, female, science fiction fan.

14. Participant 35, female, science fiction fan.

15. Participant 18, male, science fiction fan.

16. Participant 2, male.

17. All quotations in this sentence are from participant 49, female.

18. Participant 33, female.

19. Participant 47, female, science fiction fan.

20. Participant 7, female, science fiction fan.

21. Participant 55, male.

22. Participant 47, female, science fiction fan.

23. Participant 31, female.

24. Participant 13, female.

25. Participant 37, female, science fiction fan.

26. Participant 7, female, science fiction fan.

27. Participant 10, male.

28. Participant 35, female, science fiction fan.

29. Participant 32, male, science fiction fan.

30. Churchill, *Fantasies of the Master Race*, 215–228.

31. Rouse and Hanson, "American Indian Stereotyping"; Churchill, *Fantasies of the Master Race*, 239.

32. Participant 37, female, science fiction fan.

33. Here the participant was using the word "factious" as a made-up word that combines "facts" with "fiction."

34. Participant 34, female.

35. Participant 47, female, science fiction fan.

36. Participant 42, female, science fiction fan.

37. Participant 55, male.

38. Participant 7, female, science fiction fan.

39. Quoted in Churchill, *Fantasies of the Master Race*, 221.

Conclusion

1. "Robert Beltran ('Chakotay'—VOY)."

2. For an interesting look at this phenomenon, see Huhndorf, *Going Native*.

3. Cornelius, *Iroquois Corn*, xi.

Bibliography

"An Account of the first Confederacy of the Six Nations, and their present Tributaries, Dependents, and Allies, and of their Religion, and Form of Government." *The American Magazine*, December 1744, 665–669.

Adare, Sierra. "Remembering Carlisle Indian School." *News from Indian Country*, late July 2000, 10B–11B.

———. "Struggle for Control of Council at Winnemucca." *News from Indian Country*, mid-April 2000, 9A.

———. "Wasson and Other Western Shoshone Leaders Fought for Tribal Rights under the 1863 Treaty of Ruby Valley." *News from Indian Country*, mid-April 2000, 9A.

———. "Western Shoshone Chair Found Dead in Homicide Case." *News from Indian Country*, mid-March 2000, 3A.

———. *The Wyoming Guide*. Golden, CO: Fulcrum Publishing, 1999.

Adler, Linda. "Euro and African American Images of American Indians." Lecture given at Kroch Library, Cornell University, Ithaca, NY, 19 April 2000.

"Advices from America." *The British Magazine, or Monthly Repository for Gentlemen and Ladies*, August 1760, 499–502.

"American News." *The British Magazine, or Monthly Repository for Gentlemen and Ladies*, September 1760, 559.

Anderson, Myrdene, et al. "A Semiotic Perspective on the Sciences: Steps toward a New Paradigm." *Semiotica* 52 (1984): 7–47.

Axtell, James. *The European and the Indian: Essays in the Ethnohistory of Colonial North America*. New York: Oxford University Press, 1981.

Berger, Peter, and Thomas Luckmann. *The Social Construction of Reality*. London: Allen Lane, 1967.

Berkhofer, Robert F., Jr. "White Conceptions of Indians." In Washburn, *Handbook of North American Indians*, vol. 4, *History of Indian-White Relations*, 522–547.

Berkin, Carol. *First Generations: Women in Colonial America*. New York: Hill and Wang, 1997.

Bird, S. Elizabeth, ed. *Dressing in Feathers: The Construction of the Indian in American Popular Culture*, 245–261. New York: Westview Press, 1996.

———. "Not My Fantasy: The Persistence of Indian Imagery in *Dr. Quinn: Medicine Woman*." In Bird, *Dressing in Feathers*, 245–261.

Brant, Beth. "The Good Red Road." In Champagne, *Contemporary Native American Cultural Issues*, 91–101.

Brasch, Beatty. "The Y-Indian Guide and Y-Indian Princess Program." In Hirschfelder et al., *American Indian Stereotypes in the World of Children: A Reader and Bibliography*, 199–220.

Brooks, Tim, and Earle Marsh. *The Complete Directory to Prime Time Network and Cable TV Shows 1946–Present*. 7th ed. New York: Ballantine Books, 1999.

Brushia, Jodi, et al., ed. "Native Identities and Stereotypes." Focus issue, *Red Ink* 9.2/10.1 (2002).

Cassirer, Ernst. *The Philosophy of the Enlightenment.* Trans. Fritz C. A. Koelln and James P. Pettegrove. Princeton, NJ: Princeton University Press, 1951.

"Cathexis." *Star Trek: Voyager.* Directed by Kim Friedman; featuring Kate Mulgrew, Robert Beltran, Brian Markinson, and Michael Cumpsty. KMCI, Lawrence, KS, 6 September 2000.

"Chaco Canyon." National Park Service. http://www.nps.gov/chcu.

Champagne, Duane, ed. *Contemporary Native American Cultural Issues.* Walnut Creek, CA: Altamira Press, 1999.

———. *Native America: Portrait of the Peoples.* Detroit: Visible Ink Press, 1994.

Churchill, Ward. *Fantasies of the Master Race: Literature, Cinema, and the Colonization of American Indians.* Monroe, ME: Common Courage Press, 1992.

Clifton, James A., ed. *The Invented Indian: Cultural Fictions and Government Policies.* New Brunswick, NJ: Transaction Publishers, 1990.

"The Cloud." *Star Trek: Voyager.* Directed by David Livingston; featuring Kate Mulgrew, Robert Beltran, Angela Dohrmann, and Judy Geeson. KMCI, Lawrence, KS, 28 August 2000.

Coll-Garcia, C. T., E. C. Meyers, and L. Brillon. "Ethnic and Minority Parenting." In *Handbook of Parenting,* vol. 2, ed. March Bornstein, 189–209. Mahwah, NJ: Lawrence Erlbaum, 1995.

Commager, Henry Steele, and Allen Nevins, eds. *The Heritage of American.* Boston: Little, Brown, 1951.

Cooper, C. R., and J. Denner. "Theories Linking Culture and Psychology." *Annual Review of Psychology* 49 (1998): 559–584.

Cornelius, Carol. *Iroquois Corn in a Culture-Based Curriculum: A Framework for Respectfully Teaching about Cultures.* Albany: State University of New York Press, 1999.

Cotterill, R. S. *The Southern Indians: The Story of the Civilized Tribes before Removal.* Norman: University of Oklahoma Press, 1954.

Council on Interracial Books for Children. "Textbooks and Native Americans." In Hirschfelder et al., *American Indian Stereotypes in the World of Children: A Reader and Bibliography.*

Coward, John M. *The Newspaper Indian: Native American Identity in the Press, 1820–90.* Champaign: University of Illinois Press, 1999.

Cutler, Charles L. *O Brave New Words! Native American Loanwords in Current English.* Norman: University of Oklahoma Press, 1994.

Dana, Francis, Edward Wigglesforth, and Peter Thacher. "Petition of the Society for Propagating the Gospel among the Indians and Others in North America, to the Honourable the Senate, and the Honourable House of Representatives, of the Commonwealth of Massachusetts." *The American Museum, or Repository,* November 1789, 430–431.

Deloria, Vine, Jr. *God Is Red: A Native View of Religion.* 1974. Reprint, Golden, CO: Fulcrum Publishing, 1994.

"Dialogue between Mercury—An English Duelists—A North-American Savage." *The British Magazine, or Monthly Repository for Gentlemen and Ladies,* March 1760, 118–121.

Donovan, Hedley, et al., eds. *The Indians.* New York: Time-Life Books, 1973.

Dryer, Richard. *The Matter of Images: Essay on Representations.* New York: Routledge, 1993.

Evans, Sarah M. *Born for Liberty: A History of Women in America.* 2nd ed. New York: Free Press, 1997.

Feest, Christian F. "Pride and Prejudice: The Pocahontas Myth and the Pamunkey." In Clifton, *The Invented Indian: Cultural Fictions and Government Policies,* 49–70.

Ferguson, Robert A. *The American Enlightenment 1750–1820.* Cambridge, MA: Harvard University Press, 1997.

Foreman, Grant. *Indian Removal.* 1932. Reprint, Norman: University of Oklahoma Press, 1972.

Franklin, Benjamin. "Remarks on the North American Indians." *The American Museum, or Repository,* April 1789, 343–346.

Frazier, Deborah. "New Agers Damaging Artifacts They Value." *Rocky Mountain News,* 23 June 1994, 8A.

"Freedom." *Quantum Leap.* Directed by Alan J. Levi; featuring Scott Bakula, Dean Stockwell, Frank Sotonma Salsedo, and Gloria Hayes. Orig. aired on NBC, 14 February 1990.

Friar, Ralph E., and Natasha A. Friar. *The Only Good Indian . . . The Hollywood Gospel.* New York: Drama Book Specialists, 1972.

Gay, Peter. *The Enlightenment: An Interpretation.* Vol. 1, *The Rise of Modern Paganism.* New York: W. W. Norton, 1966.

Gibson, Arrel Morgan. *The American Indian: Prehistory to the Present.* Lexington, MA: D. C. Heath, 1980.

Hirschfelder, Arlene. "What's Correct? American Indian or Native American?" In Hirschfelder et al., *American Indian Stereotypes in the World of Children: A Reader and Bibliography,* 27–30.

Hirschfelder, Arlene, Paulette Fairbanks Molin, and Yvonne Wakim, eds. *American Indian Stereotypes in the World of Children: A Reader and Bibliography.* 2nd ed. Lanham, MD: Scarecrow Press, 1999.

"Historical Chronicle: Boston." *The American Magazine,* August 1745, 368–372.

"History of the Treatment of Prisoners among the American Indians." *The American Museum, or Repository,* May 1789, 468–469.

Horsman, Reginald. *Race and Manifest Destiny: The Origins of American Racial Anglo-Saxonism.* Cambridge, MA: Harvard University Press, 1981.

Huhndorf, Shari M. *Going Native: Indians in the American Cultural Imagination.* Ithaca, NY: Cornell University Press, 2001.

Huntington, Ellsworth. *The Red Man's Continent.* New Haven, CT: Yale University Press, 1919.

Jacobs, Wilbur R. "British Indian Policies to 1783." In Washburn, *Handbook of North American Indians,* vol. 4, *History of Indian-White Relations,* 5–12.

Josephy, Jr., Alvin M., Joane Nagel, and Troy Johnson, eds. *Red Power: The American Indians' Fight for Freedom.* 2nd ed. Lincoln, NE: Bison Books, 1999.

Kehoe, Alice B. "Primal Gaia: Primitivists and Plastic Medicine Men." In Clifton, *The Invented Indian: Cultural Fictions and Government Policies,* 193–209.

Kilpatrick, Jacquelyn. *Celluloid Indians: Native Americans and Film.* Lincoln, NE: Bison Books, 1999.

King, Richard, and Charles Fruehling Springwood. *Team Spirits: The Native American Mascots Controversy.* Lincoln, NE: Bison Books, 2001.

Leach, Douglas Edward. "Colonial Indian Wars." In Washburn, *Handbook of North American Indians,* vol. 4, *History of Indian-White Relations,* 128–143.

Lévi-Strauss, Claude. *Myth and Meaning: Cracking the Code of Culture.* New York: Schocken Books, 1979.

Lubber, Klaus. *Born for the Shade: Stereotypes of the Native American in United States Literature and the Visual Arts, 1779–1894.* Atlanta: Rodopi, 1994.

Lyons, Oren, Chief, and John Mohawk, eds. *Exiled in the Land of the Free: De-*

mocracy, Indian Nations, and the U.S. Constitution. Santa Fe, NM: Clear Light Publishers, 1992.

Macdonald, Andrew, Gina Macdonald, and Mary Ann Sheridan. *Shape-shifting: Images of Native Americans in Recent Popular Fiction*. Westport, CT: Greenwood Press, 2000.

Mander, Jerry. *In the Absence of the Sacred: The Failure of Technology and the Survival of the Indian Nations*. San Francisco: Sierra Book Club, 1991.

"Manner in which the American Indians carry on war—causes of war among them—encroachments on their hunting grounds,—emulation—ardour of the young warriors—spirit of revenge—their war councils and embassies." *The American Museum, or Repository*, February 1789, 147–150.

Marshall, Joseph, III. *On Behalf of the Wolf and the First Peoples*. Santa Fe, NM: Red Crane Books, 1995.

Martin, Calvin Luther. *The Way of the Human Being*. New Haven, CT: Yale University Press, 1999.

Matthiessen, Peter. *In the Spirit of Crazy Horse*. 1980. Reprint, New York: Viking Penguin, 1991.

McGaa, Ed. *Native Wisdom: Perceptions of the Natural Way*. Minneapolis: Four Directions Publishing, 1995.

Mihesuah, Devon A. *American Indians: Stereotypes and Realities*. Atlanta: Clarity Press, 1996.

Mossiker, Frances. *Pocahontas: The Life and the Legend*. 1976. New York: Da Capo Press, 1996.

Nerburn, Kent. *Neither Wolf nor Dog: On Forgotten Roads with an Indian Elder*. Novato, CA: New World Library, 1994.

Orkin, Andrew J. "One Editorial Cartoon, Two Very Different Perceptions." *Toronto Star*, 30 March 2002, A8.

"The Paradise Syndrome." *Star Trek*. Directed by Jud Taylor; featuring William Shatner, Leonard Nimoy, Sabrina Scharf, and Rudy Solari. Lawrence. KS, 28 February 2001.

Parezo, Nancy. "American Indian Stereotypes: Persistent Cultural Blindness." In Brushia et al., "Native Identities and Stereotypes," 41–49.

Perkins, Barbara, Robyn Warhol, and George Perkins. *Woman's Work: An Anthology of American Literature*. New York: McGraw-Hill, 1994.

Pewewardy, Cornel D. "Educators and Mascots: Challenging Contradictions." In *Team Spirits: The Native American Mascots Controversy*, ed. C. Richard King and Charles F. Springwood, 257–278. Lincoln, NE: University of Nebraska Press, 2001.

———. "Fluff and Feathers: Treatment of American Indians in the Literature and the Classroom." *Equity and Excellence in Education* 31.1 (1998): 69–76.

———. "I'm Not Your Indian Mascot Anymore: Countering the Assault of Indian Mascots in Schools." In Brushia et al., *Native Identities and Stereotypes*, 58–62.

———. "Recapturing Stolen Media Images: Indians Are *Not* Mascots or Logos." In Hirschfelder et al., *American Indian Stereotypes in the World of Children: A Reader and Bibliography*, 189–192.

———. "Renaming Ourselves on Our Own Terms: Race, Tribal Nations, and Representation in Education." *Indigenous Nations Studies Journal* 1.1 (2000): 11–28.

———. "Why Educators Should Not Ignore Indian Mascots." *Multicultural Perspectives* 2.1 (2000) : 3–7.

Prucha, Francis Paul, ed. *Documents of United States Indian Policy*. 3rd ed. Lincoln: University of Nebraska Press, 2000.

———. *The Great Father: The United States Government and the American Indians.* Abr. ed. Lincoln: University of Nebraska Press, 1984.

Ramirez, Susan Berry Brill de. *Contemporary American Indian Literatures and the Oral Tradition.* Tucson: University of Arizona Press, 1999.

Ranade, R. D. *Mysticism in India: The Poet-Saints of Maharashtra.* Albany: State University of New York Press, 1983.

"The Recent Events." *The Southern Banner,* 23 March 1833.

Reddicliffe, Steven, et al., eds. "Star Trek: A Timeless Guide to the Trek Universe." Special thirty-fifth anniversary tribute issue, *TV Guide,* July 2002.

Reid, John Phillip. *A Law of Blood: The Primitive Law of the Cherokee Nation.* New York: New York University Press, 1970.

Ridpath, John Clark. *History of the World: Being an Account of the Principal Events in the Career of the Human Race from the Beginnings of Civilization to the Present Time Comprising the Development of Social Institutions and the Story of All Nations from Recent and Authentic Sources.* Vol. 7. Chicago: Riverside, 1901.

"Robert Beltran ('Chakotay'—VOY)." Transcript of online chat, 4 March 1999. http://www.startrek.com/startrek/view/community/chat/archive/transcript/1210.html.

Rouse, Linda P., and Jeffery R. Hanson. "American Indian Stereotyping, Resource Competition, and Status-Based Prejudice." *American Indian Culture and Research Journal* 15.3 (1991): 1–17.

Ryan, Allan J. *The Trickster Shift: Humour and Irony in Contemporary Native Art.* Seattle: University of Washington Press, 1999.

Rydell, Robert. *All the World's a Fair: Visions of Empire at American International Expositions, 1876–1916.* Chicago: University of Chicago Press, 1984.

"Schemitzun!" *Connecticut Mashantucket Pequot.* KCPT, 15 July 2000.

Seale, Doris. "Let Us Put Our Minds Together and See What Life We Will Make for Our Children." In Slapin and Seale, *Through Indian Eyes: The Native Experience in Books for Children,* 7–12.

Seaver, James E. *A Narrative of the Life of Mrs. Mary Jemison.* 1824. Reprint, New York: Random House, 1929.

Shaughnessy, Tim. "White, Stereotypes of Indians." *Journal of American Indian Education* 17.2 (1978): 1–4.

Shimkin, Demitri B. "Eastern Shoshone." In Washburn, *Handbook of North American Indians,* vol. 4, *History of Indian-White Relations,* 310–311.

———. "Eastern Shoshone." In *Handbook of North American Indians,* vol. 11, *Great Basin,* ed. Warren L. d'Azevedo (1986), 308–335.

Sigel, I. E., A. V. McGillicuddy-DeLisi, and J. J. Goodnow, eds. *Parental Belief Systems: The Psychological Consequences for Children.* 2nd ed. Hillsdale, NJ: Lawrence Erlbaum, 1992.

Slapin, Beverly. Introduction to Slapin and Seale, *Through Indian Eyes: The Native Experience in Books for Children,* 1–4.

Slapin, Beverly, and Doris Seale. "The Bloody Trail of Columbus Day." In Slapin and Seale, *Through Indian Eyes: The Native Experience in Books for Children,* 5–6.

———, eds. *Through Indian Eyes: The Native Experience in Books for Children.* Los Angeles: University of California, 1998.

Smith, Linda Tuhiwai. *Decolonizing Methodologies: Research and Indigenous Peoples.* New York: Zed Books, 1999.

Strickland, Rennard. *Tonto's Revenge: Reflections on American Indian Culture and Policy.* Albuquerque: University of New Mexico Press, 1997.

Takaki, Ronald. *A Different Mirror: A History of Multicultural America*. New York: Little, Brown, 1993.

"Tattoo." *Star Trek: Voyager*. Directed by Alexander Singer; featuring Kate Mulgrew, Robert Beltran, Henry Darrow, and Richard Fancy. Orig. aired on 6 November 1995.

Taylor, Annette M. "Cultural Heritage in *Northern Exposure*." In Bird, *Dressing in Feathers*, 229–244.

Taylor, Drew Hayden. *Funny, You Don't Look Like One: Observations from a Blue-Eyed Ojibway*. Penticton, British Columbia: Theytus Books, 1998.

Taylor, R. W. "The Effects of Economic and Social Stressors on Parenting and Adolescent Adjustment in African-American Families." In *Social and Emotional Adjustment and Family Relations in Ethnic Minority Families*, ed. R. W. Taylor and M. C. Wang, 35–52. Mahwah, NJ: Lawrence Erlbaum, 1997.

"Test of a Warrior." *The Adventures of Superman*. Directed by George Blair; featuring George Reeves, Ralph Moody, Francis McDonald, and Maurice Jara. Orig. aired 1954.

Usner, Daniel. "American Indian History 1500–1850." Lecture given at Cornell University, Ithaca, NY, 10 February 1999.

Utley, Robert. "Indian-Unites States Military Situation, 1848–1891." In *Handbook of North American Indians*, vol. 4, *History of Indian-White Relations*, 163–184.

Venables, Robert W. *Crowded Wilderness: American Indians, the United States, and the Five Hundred Year War for Indian America*. Ithaca, NY: Cornell University, 1999.

Vickers, Scott B. *Native American Identities: From Stereotype to Archetype in Art and Literature*. Albuquerque: University of New Mexico Press, 1998.

Wade, Mason. "French Indian Policies." In Washburn, *Handbook of North American Indians*, vol. 4, *History of Indian-White Relations*, 20–28.

Wagner, Roy. *The Invention of Culture*. Englewood Cliffs, NJ: Prentice-Hall, 1975.

Ward, Carol, Elon Stander, and Yodit Soloman. "Resistance through Healing among American Indian Women." In *A World Systems Reader*, ed. Thomas D. Hall. New York: Rowman and Littlefield, 2000.

Warry, Wayne. *Unfinished Dreams: Community Healing and the Reality of Aboriginal Self-Government*. Toronto: University of Toronto Press, 1998.

Washburn, Wilcomb E., ed. *Handbook of North American Indians*. Vol. 4, *History of Indian-White Relations*. 20 vols. Washington, DC: Smithsonian Institution, 1988.

Weeks, Lyman Horace, and Edwin M. Bacon, eds. *An Historical Digest of the Provincial Press 1689–1783*. Boston: Society for Americana, 1891.

Whitt, Laurie Anne. "Cultural Imperialism and the Marketing of Native America." In Champagne, *Contemporary Native American Cultural Issues*, 169–192.

Wilson, James. *The Earth Shall Weep: A History of Native America*. New York: Grove Press, 1998.

Wilson, L. C., and D. R. William. "Issues in the Quality of Data on Minority Groups." In *Studying Minority Adolescents: Conceptual, Methodological, and Theoretical Issues*, ed. Vonnie McLoyd and Laurence Steinberg, 237–250. Mahwah, NJ: Lawrence Erlbaum, 1998.

Wright, J. Leitch, Jr. *The Only Land They Knew: American Indians in the Old South*. Lincoln: University of Nebraska Press, 1999.

Wright, Ronald. *Stolen Continents: The Americas through Indian Eyes since 1492*. New York: Houghton Mifflin, 1992.

Index